Twayne's United States Authors Series

EDITOR OF THIS VOLUME

David J. Nordloh

University of Indiana

Finley Peter Dunne

TUSAS 402

Finley Peter Dunne

FINLEY PETER DUNNE

By GRACE ECKLEY

Drake University

TWAYNE PUBLISHERS

A DIVISION OF G. K. HALL & CO., BOSTON

Published in 1981 by Twayne Publishers,
A Division of G. K. Hall & Co.
All Rights Reserved

Printed on permanent/durable acid-free paper and bound
in the United States of America

First Printing

Frontispiece drawing of Finley Peter Dunne
courtesy of Elmer Ellis

Library of Congress Cataloging in Publication Data

Eckley, Grace.
    Finley Peter Dunne.
    (Twayne's United States authors series ; 402)
    Bibliography: p. 158-61
    Includes indexes.
    1.   Dunne, Finley Peter, 1867-1936—Criticism and
interpretation.
    PS3507.U6755Z57   818'.5207   80-20446
    ISBN 0-8057-7295-2

OK √

To
Elmer Ellis
Barbara Schaaf
Richard Crowe
Philip Dunne
and all other followers of Mr. Dooley

Contents

About the Author

Grace Eckley is Professor of English at Drake University where she has taught since 1968. She received an A.B. degree from Mount Union College (1955), an M.A. degree from Case Western Reserve University (1964), and the Ph.D. degree from Kent State University (1970).

Dr. Eckley teaches courses in graduate and undergraduate British literature, in world mythology, and in science fiction. She has published mainly in contemporary Irish literature and specializes in James Joyce's *Finnegans Wake.* Her books are *Benedict Kiely* for the Twayne English Authors Series; *Edna O'Brien* for the Bucknell University Irish Writers Series; *Narrator and Character in Finnegans Wake,* co-authored with Michael Begnal, published by Bucknell University Press; and *Padding Joyce's Footsteps,* on folklore and mythology in the work of James Joyce.

Preface

My own interest in Finley Peter Dunne began with James Joyce's novel *Finnegans Wake* in which, in order to analyze the Duke of Wellington passage, I had to work backward to Dooley and Hennessy. Joyce was so enamored of Mr. Dooley that he even retained Dooley's pronunciation, "Hinnessy." Then I remembered, from the vague caverns of the mind, that Joyce had written also a poem called "Dooleysprudence." I was launched on an investigation which took me to other scholars in the field: Elmer Ellis, Barbara C. Schaaf, Charles Fanning, and, of course, Philip Dunne, famous screenwriter son of Finley Peter Dunne. Over all beamed Chicago folklorist Richard Crowe, a city planner who knows every crack and recess of that great city where Dunne began.

Was it Will Rogers who said that everything he knew he got from the newspapers? He followed after Finley Peter Dunne's "Mr. Dooley," who began many a monologue with "I see be th' pa-apers." And Dooley commented frequently on the variety of lifestyles made available through such reading. The device provided the means by which Finley Peter Dunne, widely traveled and received in the homes of titans of business, finance, and government, and intimate friend of United States presidents, could present his personal experiences in the homely philosophy of a Chicago bartender who seldom moved far from "Archey Road" but who remembered his Irish origins. The philosophy worked, as did the essays, for Dunne in his time became, as his son Philip wrote, the "moral censor of the nation." The "Mr. Dooley" song has a line to this effect: "And if he even sneezes they will get an extra out." The first chapter of the present book sets forth the biographical backgrounds.

How much of his native origins Dunne was serious about has become a matter of conjecture among contemporary scholars. To many of the Chicago Irish, Dunne *was* Chicago Irish, the epitome of the immigrant in primitive America rapidly changing to industrialized America. To others, Mr. Dooley's Irishness was a post on which Dunne could conveniently lean for independence and skepticism of viewpoint. It made him, so to speak, a benevolent outsider and a mainstream critic—an unbeatable combination. Chapter 2 discusses the Irish content of the essays.

The most erroneous and superficial judgment any human being can make about another is that the person is "simple" when instead he has a talent for conveying profundities in simple language. Finley Peter Dunne saw the Irish of Archey Road as "simple like the air or th' deep sea," having a breadth and depth of understanding which the philosopher trained in teleology could well emulate. In the third chapter, in placing Dunne in relationship to other humorists, I dispute the widely-held critical theory that Dunne's appeal was to the cult of the ignorant; instead his appeal resided in that most fundamental of human sympathies, the recognition of a keen fellow mind.

The Spanish-American War sprang Dunne into national and international fame, and the fourth chapter covers his war essays, beginning with the Spanish-American, continuing through the Boer War, then the Russo-Japanese War, and on to World War I. In the background also was the Civil War. In this chapter I have continued somewhat my argument from the previous chapter that the success of Dunne's essays was based on knowledge and the reader's recognition of facts; and I have analyzed the backgrounds of one of Dunne's most famous essays, "On the Destruction of Cervera's Fleet," to show what kinds of wide-ranging facts (and how many of them) Dunne utilized in a single piece.

Chapter 5 covers the remaining essays, those dealing with the turbulent times of peace and such intimate concerns as sports, women's suffrage, and national politics. Some surprises may be found here. For example, did Dunne suggest the title for a story by Daniel Keyes, the "Flowers for Algernon," when he wrote of strewing roses for Algernon?

Chapter 6 attempts to suggest the long-range appeal of Dunne's essays through some lively and debatable topics for the present day, as well as the continuing presence of Mr. Dooley in such works as that of James Joyce, Tom Stoppard's play *Travesties*, a video tape for the Democratic National Convention, and among Chicago historians.

Much scholarship needs yet to be accomplished in regard to

Finley Peter Dunne's Mr. Dooley. While preparing this book, I have been continually dismayed at the frustrating effects of the popularizing of Dunne's essays; many of the collections, even when the collector was busy retrieving essays from now-microfilmed newspapers and magazines, fail to include such scholarly apparatus as the source—date and title of the publication—for the article. The sequence of the essays and the date of writing become important for several reasons, not the least of which is the probable inspiration and hence the final outcome of the subject. Moreover, such collectors, no doubt needing to accommodate to a publisher who would accept the book on its popular appeal rather than its scholarly apparatus, have totally overlooked the fact that their work may be subject to suspicion in regard to its accuracy. Certainly Mr. Dooley was so popular in Dunne's own day that many writers tried their hand at writing Mr. Dooley essays. The suspicion of illegitimacy, then, hangs over their reproductions from obscure magazines. I cannot rest content with work on Dunne until all the essays are dated, labeled, and arranged in proper sequence. Some collectors and publishers have used different titles for the same essays. I would like to see the scholarship catch up with the popularity.

Another problem that should be mentioned is the Dunne-Dooley relationship, revealed occasionally when critics say, "Dooley writes." The question remains whether Dunne speaks through Dooley in Dunne's own voice or whether Dooley has a voice separate from that of Dunne. Confounding the issue, I believe, is the fact that both are true. I have tried to solve the problem by saying, "Dunne writes" and "Dooley says."

The space requirements of the Twayne series have led me to consider carefully the space devoted to each essay. Dunne's biographer, Elmer Ellis, estimated that Dunne wrote over 700 dialect essays, of which about one-third were published in eight books during Dunne's lifetime. I believe I have commented on all of these anthologized essays, at least by naming them in a subject-oriented background, so that any reader may determine where the essay need be consulted for further study. Having been annoyed by lack of scholarly apparatus in works I consulted, I have carefully in my context (and unobtrusively, I hope) cited parenthetically the volume or other source of the particular essay being discussed so that my readers can find it for further consultation. The number of anthologized essays, primarily because of the work of Chicagoans Barbara C. Schaaf and Charles Fanning, has been somewhat increased since Elmer Ellis's writing.

Dunne's first three books, collections of his newspaper articles, were best sellers in 1898, 1899, and 1900. From those years through the 1920s his essays were popular for various recitals, including those of adults as well as school boy elocution. More recently, among the generation of Americans who were in high school in the 1940s are many who remember the "Mr. Dooley" essays featured in their literature texts. College students of the 1950s found Dooley observations in their history texts. Indeed, Dunne's biographer, Elmer Ellis, began his research in Dunne's life after finding that Dunne's insights aided his teaching of American history. During the first half of the twentieth century, many people—without attempting to imitate the Irish-American dialect of the Dooley pieces—quoted his epigrams, of which one of the most famous is "No matter whether the Constitution follows the flag or not, the Supreme Court follows the election returns." His comments covered almost everything, and his readers could pick a favorite quotation to fit their own philosophies or predicaments: "Would I send a boy to college? Well, at the age when a boy is fit to be in college I wouldn't have him around the house."

Often Dunne delighted his readers with unexpected linkings of remote endeavors: "I know a lot about children. Not being an author, I'm a great critic." As a writer he had many comments on his own discipline: "The further you get away from any period the better you can write about it. You aren't subject to interruptions by people that were there." Often a single adjective or a picturesque verb proved a brilliant stroke against a homely thought, as on the familiar topic of reverence for age: "Many a man that couldn't direct you to the drugstore on the corner when he was thirty will get a respectful hearing when age has further impaired his mind."

Dunne's success in his own time depended on immediacy; to write of a topic discontinued or overexposed would have deprived him of his audience. He had, moreover, a talent for discerning inaccuracy, hypocrisy, or ulterior motive. But his successful topicality means that the humor and precision of many of the essays may be lost to contemporary readers; therefore, in this book I have tried to sketch sufficient historical background to provide recognition—or reminders—of the merit of Dunne's observations. In contrast with this topicality, however, many of the essays have lasting and even prophetic powers. For example, the English-Irish conflict renewed in 1968 in North Ireland has been based on a steady erosion of English resistance to Irish independence. Dunne, in an essay collected in the 1906 volume, wrote, "England will niver free Ireland, but some day, if we make it inthrestin' enough f'r her she'll have to free England iv Ireland."

The essays reveal, also, that social consciousness in regard to sensitive issues such as minorities has changed much since Dunne's time; but far in advance of his time, Dunne criticized the pushing of Indians off the face of the land so that, he said, they must inhabit a diving bell in the Pacific, and the confining of blacks to the "Colored Supplement" of the newspapers. The latter half of the twentieth century, experienced with two wars and the continuing threat of war, can well apppeciate his wish that "it could be fixed up so that the men that start the war could do the fighting." Not to obscure issues or to be selective in Dunne's favor, the attempt of this volume is to present an overview of the full range of Dunne's topics.

Some mysteries remain surrounding the loss of Dunne's papers. His sister Charlotte, to whom he entrusted many private thoughts in letters, was killed by a burglar in her own home. The movement of the rest of the family has apparently meant that many papers were misplaced. For this reason, the biography by Elmer Ellis—who did careful research in parish and school records and among contemporaries and relatives, when those were still available—remains as the only guide to much now-lost material. I am grateful for his book *Mr. Dooley's America*, whose biographical materials I have reproduced in abbreviated form in my first chapter, and for his personal consultation.

The Democratic National Committee entrusted their video tape to me and sent it through the mails; the Chicago Historical Society provided copies of their materials on Dunne, including the Grant Richards letters. Philip Dunne has been more than cooperative in sharing his views and information and has given permission to quote from his correspondence and from *Mr. Dooley Remembers,* which he edited.

Other than those "followers of Mr. Dooley" who have gained my lasting appreciation and with whom I have a sense of fellowship, there are several librarians at Drake University's Cowles Library of whom I can sincerely, though tritely, say, "without whom. . . ."

GRACE ECKLEY

Drake University

Chronology

1867   Peter Dunne born July 10 in Chicago, a twin of John Dunne (who died in infancy), fifth of seven surviving children of Peter Dunne (born in Queens County, Ireland) and Ellen Finley Dunne (born in Kilkenny, Ireland).

1875   Began reading Macaulay's *History of England* aloud to his mother.

1884   Graduated, last in a class of over fifty, from West Division High School; began work for *Chicago Telegram* in June, and later for *Chicago Daily News* as sports reporter.

1886   Added his mother's name, Finley, to his own.

1888   Worked for *Chicago Times* as political reporter and writer of political editorials; promoted to city editor, solved Cronin murder mystery.

1889   Began work with *Chicago Daily Tribune* as general reporter.

1890   Became editor of Sunday edition, and moved to *Chicago Herald*, specializing in political reporting.

1892   Covered political conventions and was transferred to the *Chicago Evening Post,* in which, on December 4, he published the first Colonel McNeery piece; also worked for *Chicago Sunday Post.*

1893   First Martin Dooley piece published in *Sunday Post,* October 7.

1895   *Chicago Times-Herald* merger.

1896   Hennessy introduced as character in Dooley pieces.

1897   Editorial writer for *Chicago Daily Journal.*

1898   *Boston Globe* began reprinting Dooley pieces; other papers soon followed; *Post* clippings from 1895 on, with some *Journal* pieces, made the first book, *Mr. Dooley in Peace and in War,* published by Small, Maynard of Boston.

1899   *Mr. Dooley in the Hearts of His Countrymen. What Dooley Says,* a British pirated edition, brought out in

Chicago by Kazmar. Dunne wrote Molly Donahue dialect pieces for *Ladies' Home Journal* and Chicago pieces for *Saturday Evening Post*. Traveled to England, Paris, and Ireland.

1900 Moved to New York; visited Mediterranean. *Mr. Dooley's Philosophy.*

1901 *Mr. Dooley's Opinions.* Dunne traveled to Mexico. Popular song, the "Mr. Dooley March," published.

1902 Trip to London, Paris, Florence, Rome, audience with Pope Leo XIII. Wrote editorials for *Collier's Weekly*. Married Margaret Abbott on December 9. *Observations by Mr. Dooley.* Became editor of the *New York Morning Telegraph.*

1903 Son Finley Peter Dunne, Jr., born.

1904 Death of William C. Whitney in February; Dunne severed connections with *New York Morning Telegraph.*

1906 Part owner and editor of the *American Magazine*, writing dialect essays and "In the Interpreter's House" editorials. *Dissertations by Mr. Dooley.*

1908 Son Philip Dunne born.

1910 Twins Margaret and Leonard Dunne born. *Mr. Dooley Says.*

1911 Wrote essays "From the Bleachers" for the *Metropolitan.*

1913 Left the editorial position at the *American Magazine*, continuing to write "In the Interpreter's House" essays until 1915; also joined *Collier's Weekly* as editor.

1917 Edited the *Pioneer Bulletin;* became editor-in-chief of *Collier's.*

1919 Ended editorship of *Collier's* with its sale. *Mr. Dooley on Making a Will and Other Necessary Evils.*

1923 Ill health, two operations.

1924 Selected and shortened old Dooley articles for the Bell Syndicate; these reprints ran two years.

1926 Wrote new Dooley essays weekly for *Liberty* over a period of six months.

1927 Payne Whitney died, leaving Dunne half a million dollars.

1936 Died of cancer, April 24.

1938 *Mr. Dooley at His Best,* edited by Elmer Ellis.

1941 *Mr. Dooley's America: A Life of Finley Peter Dunne* by Elmer Ellis.

1963 *Mr. Dooley Remembers: The Informal Memoirs of Finley Peter Dunne*, edited by Philip Dunne.

CHAPTER 1

"I See Be th' Pa-apers"

THE highlights of Finley Peter Dunne's life, like those of many other lives, have been summarized dramatically and questioned thoughtfully. According to the exaggerated story, he was born of lower-class Irish parents in Chicago. He was not: his parents were middle class, with subscriptions to magazines in the home and with a good supply of scholarly books, from which, at the age of eight, Peter Dunne read aloud to his mother one of her favorites, Thomas Babington Macaulay's *History of England*. Although William Thackeray instead of Macaulay soon became the child's favorite, this reading indicates precocity by both yesterday's and today's standards and certainly contradicts reports that Dunne was a dunce in school. Staying in school seemed a matter of plodding indifference, however, and Dunne was known to graduate at the bottom of his class. Not to be sent to college seemed a foregone conclusion, but Dunne's brilliance blossomed and his salary improved commensurably when he began work with Chicago papers. As a sports reporter, he solved the Cronin murder mystery, but rumor in Chicago to this day continues speculation that the real killer was never found. Dunne adopted his mother's maiden name and became famous as Finley Peter Dunne, the creator of "Mr. Dooley." He earned the confidence of President Theodore Roosevelt even while continuing to satirize him in the Dooley essays, and he married into high society. His sons attended private eastern schools and Harvard. It is a life story to be envied, a rise-to-riches truism of the American dream.

I   The Chicago Backgrounds

Finley Peter Dunne's biographer, Elmer Ellis, reports these facts of Dunne's life; and, because of loss of records through moving and disregard, probably no source will improve on that original, mistitled *Mr. Dooley's America* (1941).[1] The sketch of Dunne's childhood indicates a lackadaisical high-school career in which, nevertheless, the character of Dunne emerges as known in later years around the men's clubs and through his career as journalist. Having written in his teen years a play, "The Chestnuts," for home performance, later famous for his witticisms both in and out of print, Dunne had interests at West Division High School centered in the debate club and in the high-school newspaper. In fact, he and a friend published a handwritten newspaper containing not only school topics but also editorials against the protective tariff. His remarkable memory was exhibited in a class he disliked—Latin—when, amid a history of failure, one day he astonished the teacher by reciting and translating a long passage from Vergil. The inconsistency of his scholarship derived from independence of viewpoint which promoted an obvious indifference to daily routine; but the three interests and qualities here exhibited—oral skills, journalism, and memory—combined with a sturdy independence of viewpoint, no doubt explain much of the success of the Dooley essays.

Whether these qualities can be called peculiarly "Irish"—and what role Dunne's Irish origins played in the Dooley essays—continues to be debated. His father, Peter, a carpenter, had moved from Queens County, Ireland, at the age of six; his mother had been born in Kilkenny, Ireland, and could not have lived there long. She was twenty-five years younger than her husband; both were Irish Catholics. She, more than her husband, was equipped to respond to and encourage the early verbal and literary talents of her son Peter. To her Peter read Macaulay's *History of England* aloud while he was attending Scammon Public School; but she died of tuberculosis before he finished high school in 1884. It was only two years after graduation that Peter honored her by attaching her maiden name, Finley, to his own as middle name; in 1888 he reversed the order and made her name his first. As evidence of his attachment to her and her devotion to learning, he was the only one among his brothers (the others were Patrick and Leonard) to attend high school. Of his sisters, Amelia, Katherine, Mary, and Charlotte, it was Amelia who became most famous in education, exhibiting some of the family talent for literature and drama, becoming a school principal, and having after her death a public school—the Amelia Dunne Hookway School—named in her honor. Family

finances permitted sending Peter to college, but his father
deemed his poor high-school record—he was, as reported,
graduated last in his class—sufficient reason to send him instead
to work.

As a journalist Dunne began office work at the age of sixteen
and at a salary of five dollars per week. The mid-1880s were an
exciting time when Chicago was booming from the construction
of the Illinois-Michigan Canal, which, as an employment
opportunity, contributed to the tripling of the Irish population so
that it comprised one-fifth of the city's total. Among Dunne's
friends in his early days as a journalist was the policeman John
Shea, whom he considered the best among capable officers of
peace, and of whom he wrote in his memoirs, "Scores of times I
have rambled with Jack Shea through the night streets of
Chicago, talking ancient Irish poetry, about which he knew a
great deal and I was sort of dab."[2] Cuffing a ruffian and sending
him away in a patrol wagon, Jack Shea would return to an
interrupted discussion, saying, "Now what was it you were saying
about Finn MacCool being a fabulous and not a historic
character?" (*Remembers*, 63). Another friend was William
Pinkerton of the famous detective agency, with whom Dunne
often discussed policemen and police work.

The scenes Dunne witnessed around the city would be written
into tender essays such as one called "On the Popularity of
Firemen," reprinted in *Mr. Dooley in the Hearts of His
Countrymen* (1899) describing Casey's risking his life for twenty
years, then to plan his resignation, only to die in the last fire. In
Dooley's voice, the experiences of Dunne were always personal;
and in his essay "'Their Excellencies the Police," in the same
volume, Dunne by way of Dooley shows how he knew the life of
policemen, as well as firemen, to be hard and rigorous. Dooley
recounts an experience of being accosted by a policeman after
curfew but failing to recognize the policeman as long as he
speaks courteously. Dooley threatens his unknown enemy's very
life, only to know him at last as an officer when he is threatened
in return.

Police work enabled Dunne to promote himself from errand
boy to writer at the *Telegram*, and from there, still in his first
year and only seventeen, to reporter for the *Chicago Daily News*
in response to a summons from its editor, Henry Ten Eyck White,
who began immediately training him for editorial writing. To his

reports, Dunne added touches of satirical wit, especially when writing about politics and public figures. In 1885 and 1886 Chicago boasted championship baseball teams; and in the spring of 1887 the evening *News* began printing baseball news. In 1887 both Dunne and his close friend and companion Horatio Seymour of the *Herald* were using the term "southpaw" in writing colorful coverage of Chicago White Stocking baseball games, and Dunne was credited with coining the term. During his travels to other cities with the baseball team, Dunne continued to comment on politics and personalities. He accepted, in 1888, an offer as political reporter for the *Chicago Times,* and wrote political editorials in keeping with its Democratic endorsements. Covering the political conventions, he wrote so well that he restored the flagging circulation of the *Times* and was promoted to city editor.

Here Dunne achieved his greatest coup as reporter. When Dr. Patrick Cronin disappeared, Dunne acted on a tip from a friend in a Chicago restaurant and began charting every move of Daniel Coughlin, the very detective who had been placed in charge of the investigation. A fellow reporter, Joe Dunlop, one of those split-shift journalists with underworld involvements, named the location where Dan Coughlin had hired a horse and thus provided the missing link. The chief investigator of the crime was soon tried for murder. Perhaps still-circulating stories that Coughlin was not the real criminal stem from doubts at the trial, where one juryman held out. Given life imprisonment, Coughlin later appealed the "guilty" verdict, and the State Supreme Court released him; but Dunne remained convinced of Coughlin's guilt, as his memoirs indicate (*Remembers,* 68–82).

Because of difficulties with the management of the *Times,* in the late summer of 1889 its editor, James J. West, was dismissed, and Dunne as city editor was forced out along with him. The next day, however, Dunne was hired by the *Chicago Daily Tribune* as general reporter and, early in January 1890, became editor of the Sunday edition. Later the same year, he moved to the *Chicago Herald* to specialize in political reporting. Elmer Ellis details Dunne's growing disenchantment with routine reporting (*America,* 41–45), although highlights were his coverage of the 1892 Republican convention in Minneapolis and the Democratic convention in Chicago. Dunne concluded the report of a rousing Republican speech with typical cocky satire: "Then all the people put on their hats and went out to see what news had come from Gettysburg, where a terrible battle is still raging" (*America*, 46).

Dunne's activities thus far had brought him into contact with many leaders of politics and journalism, including some who achieved lasting fame, like Eugene Field and Theodore Dreiser. Ellis chronicles those names with great care and provides a list of the members of the Whitechapel Club, the first of gentlemen's clubs of which Dunne became a member (see *America*, 47–54). Formed in 1889 when the gentlemen were discussing the Cronin case, the club, according to Ellis, continued to foster a Bohemian atmosphere, Rabelaisian wit, and radical politics. Among its members, Dunne became "the most expert of all in the gentle art of stripping a stuffed shirt of its covering, of gently pricking a balloon of windy conceit" (*America*, 51).

After the conventions, Dunne was transferred to the *Chicago Evening Post* (owned by the *Herald*) and given charge of the editorial page. In these offices he became acquainted with Mary Ives Abbott, a book reviewer and popular dinner guest, who improved Dunne's social outlook. Through his writing and his contacts, his importance increased and, with coverage of the World's Columbian Exposition in Chicago in the summer of 1893, Dunne was appointed a representative of the city on many festive occasions (see *America*, 56). At the same time his editor, Cornelius McAuliff, appreciated Dunne's wit and humor and gave him editorial freedoms, out of which grew serious editorials with humorous content and, eventually, the Dooley essays. At first opposed to dialect writing (see *America*, 64), Dunne responded to McAuliff's request that he write a humorous piece for each issue of a new Sunday edition of the *Post;* the assignment produced "Frank's Visit to Grover," about an Irishman's report of the visit of Frank Lawler to President Grover Cleveland concerning a post-office appointment.

Dunne, many years later in *Mr. Dooley at His Best* (1938), described the origin of his Irish dialect pieces in the person of one James McGarry, who kept a public house on Dearborn Street near the *Chicago Tribune* office. Dunne reported that McGarry had been born in County Roscommon, Ireland; and later Dunne retained this point of origin for Mr. Dooley. McGarry's characteristic witticisms became legend; and, because Dunne was inspired by McGarry's example, biographies of him take on a peculiar character. Anecdote gives way to quotation; for the peculiar flavor of the witticism, whoever functions as Dunne's speaker, makes anything other than direct quotation a form of reductionism.

The second dialect piece that Dunne wrote for the *Sunday Post* became the origin, as he later recalled, of the Dooley essays. Dunne heard McGarry comment on the death of the financier Jay Gould (December 2, 1892) and quoted McGarry, in the fictional name of Colonel McNeary, in the essay published the following Sunday. In this essay Dunne added the name of John J. McKenna, a real person, a "Republican from the Democratic stronghold of Bridgeport on Archer Avenue," a small-time politician who frequently baited McGarry. Elmer Ellis writes, "As the Dooley essays developed, McKenna became the one active character unquestionably drawn from life and traveling under his own name. The inactive characters were also real. Casey was McGarry's late barkeeper, Gavin was a well-known undertaker, and Boyle was the proprietor of the popular chophouse near by" (*America*, 69). Dunne changed the spelling to McNeery, which did not disguise the identity of McGarry; and the essays gained popularity through their recognizable characters who commented on politics and the World's Fair. When the experimental journal form of the *Sunday Post* was discontinued in 1893, the essays were continued in the Saturday edition of the daily. In September, however, McGarry found his identification in politics, often contrary to those of some of his customers, becoming somewhat uncomfortable; and Dunne was forced to drop the name McNeery.

To accommodate McGarry, Dunne changed the name of his protagonist to Mr. Dooley and changed the location of the pub from Dearborn Street to Archer Avenue and suburban Bridgeport, where the "shanty Irish" lived whom Dunne in the preface to his first book described as "a simple people! 'Simple, says ye,' remarked Mr. Dooley. 'Simple like th' air or th' deep sea'" (*Peace,* ix). Regarding the prototype of Mr. Dooley, Elmer Ellis concludes, "Dooley was compounded of the qualities of many real men, not the least of whom was Peter Dunne" (*America*, 79).

Good work must be well researched, and Dunne made the rounds of the pubs to gather additional materials. As a result, Ellis notes, many of the pieces contain tragedy and pathos as well as satire and comic humor (see *America,* 81). At the same time, Dunne as editorialist continued to write seriously against corruption. But other papers, and other writers, were publishing serious materials; these were commonplace. With the creation of Mr. Dooley, Dunne provided something different—essays the populace could memorize and recite for social and educational events, and quote in ordinary conversation. One of the most frequently recited essays concerned a mother whose beloved son was arrested.

James W. Scott in 1895 bought the *Post* and *Herald* and united them with the *Times*; but the death of Scott just two weeks after the purchase threw the paper into the hands of Herman Kohlsaat, dedicated to making William McKinley president. The change from Democratic partisanship to what Kohlsaat called "independent" forced changes in Dunne's position, and his editorials were now strictly serious. His wit and humor could be exercised now only in the Dooley pieces. After the political conventions of 1896, which Dunne covered for the *Times-Herald,* and after the campaign was over, Dunne changed the name of Dooley's confidant to Malachi Hennessy, making him, as Ellis writes, "pseudoanonymous" and leaving John McKenna a person only occasionally mentioned. In the winter of 1897–98 Dunne went to work for the *Chicago Journal,* where he restored humor and satire to his editorials.

With the mounting crises leading to the Spanish-American War, the fame of Mr. Dooley spread. Mr. Dooley's chief sources for his witticisms were the newspapers which Dunne served and read, so that "I see be th' pa-apers" became a frequent opening. The 1890s were exciting for the exposés of corruption by journalists whose papers competed for circulation on the basis of scoops. Dunne, however, was not always supportive of his craft and his colleagues and frequently criticized their coverage, especially because it fostered the war. In fact, some of his Spanish-American War essays have an antinewspaper slant. In the preface to the first collection, *Mr. Dooley in Peace and in War* (1898), Dunne wrote of Dooley, "He reads the newspapers with solemn care, heartily hates them, and accepts all they print for the sake of drowning Hennessy's rising protests against his logic."

Although scholars differ on which essay contributed most to making Dunne famous (Charles Fanning credits the essay "On

His Cousin George," about Admiral Dewey at Manila,[3] and
Elmer Ellis cites "On the Destruction of Cervera's Fleet" as "the
piece that made Mr. Dooley a national hero almost overnight"
[*America*, 113]), the qualities which endeared the essays to the
reading public may be observed in the best of these, collected by
Dunne in that first book.

Mr. Dooley has strong personal dignity and self-command,
befitting his advanced years and steady occupation. Of the
president's visit he says, "There's Prisidint Mack at th' Aud-
jiotoroom, an' here's Prisidint Dooley at nine-double-naught-
nine, an' th' len'th iv th' sthreet between thim. Says he, 'Come
over to th' hotel an' see me.' Says I, 'if ye find ye'ersilf thrun fr'm
a ca'ar in me neighborhood, dhrop in.' An' there ye ar're" (*Peace*,
82). He is known for his keenness of mind and wit, his
intelligence spans the world; like Thoreau in Concord, Dooley
travels much in his tavern. One of his techniques, a kind of
psychological reductionism, consistently places the strong man
and the victorious at a disadvantage. "Here's th' pitchers iv
candydates I pulled down fr'm th' windy, an' jus' knowin' they're
here makes me that nervous f'r th' contints iv th' cash dhrawer
I'm afraid to tur'rn me back f'r a minyit. I'm goin' to throw thim
out in th' back yard" (*Peace*, 87). Among his inventions—new
words or new uses of ordinary words, or ordinary words
ingeniously misapplied so that they sound right—he made many
puns, approximations ("Porter Ricky" for Puerto Rico), exag-
gerations (a "hurricane of applause"), and flights of eloquence.

With his newspaper, the *Chicago Journal*, editorially opposed
to the McKinley administration, Dunne's use of the fond term
"Mack" for referring to the president softened the tone of much
criticism. Regarding his father's politics, Philip Dunne writes,

Though he wrote as a nonpartisan, Peter Dunne was personally a man
of decided and often partisan views, which he didn't mind expressing.
He only refused to wear a label. His fundamental sympathies were with
the Democratic Party. Given his background in Irish Chicago and his
basic liberalism this was inevitable. Mr. Dooley, true to his character,
was always identified as a Democrat, even when making fun of
Democrats.
    But in middle life many of my father's associations were Republican.
(*Remembers*, 104)

Dunne put together *Mr. Dooley in Peace and in War,* which came out in November of 1898, with clippings from the *Post* and from the *Journal.* Dunne, concerned about income, watched the sales eagerly, noticing which stores displayed it to advantage and where the most copies were being sold. The editors of *Chicago History,* commenting with some humor on this phase of Dunne's fledgling authorship, write about the letters in their files, "Most marked of all the beginning author's attitudes is his propensity to forget that several dozen books are published daily, and to excoriate booksellers for not being exclusively concerned with his own."[4] Elmer Ellis, however, writes that "the book was selling at a steady rate of ten thousand copies a month, and it remained on the bestseller lists for a year—remained there, in fact, until a second collection of the essays appeared to destroy the first's monopoly of the market for Mr. Dooley's remarks" *America,* 120). The book made Dunne a celebrity and, writes Ellis, "As the newer Dooley essays were appearing in the papers, Secretary Gage was reading them at the meetings of the President's Cabinet" (*America,* 122). This marked the beginning of a trend, for Philip Dunne writes, "The articles were read aloud at the cabinet meetings of three Presidents. The public figures of his day thought twice before they embarked on any undertaking or uttered any important statement. They asked themselves first what Mr. Dooley would have to say about it and therefore prudently tempered their actions and their words. To borrow his own phrase, 'The Eye was on them'" (*Remembers,* 103).

The year 1899 marked the beginning of Dunne's national and international fame. He sold *Harper's Weekly* reprint rights along with the newspapers; promised a dialect series featuring an Irish lass, Molly Donahue, for the *Ladies' Home Journal,* and another series on Chicago for the *Saturday Evening Post;* he was still writing for the *Chicago Journal* while he prepared a second collection of Dooley essays for publication in a book; and he departed for a trip abroad in May, to return in September.

Grant Richards in London had brought out an unauthorized edition of Dunne's first book. Dunne's correspondence with Herbert Small reveals his resentment of this "arch pirate" who, Dunne wrote on March 21, 1899, by this time "is afraid of disagreeable notoriety as a thief." The pirate received an urgent visit from Dunne, and he did arrange a royalty on subsequent books. Dunne, however, had already written a satiric dedication for his second book, explaining his resentment of their "republishing an American book without solicitation on the author's part" (*Hearts,* vii).

En route in New York Dunne met Richard Harding Davis at a banquet among journalists meeting in Dunne's honor; and the next day, May 11, 1899, "the *New York Journal* featured the dinner with [F. B.] Opper's cartoons of Davis and Dunne" (*America,* 126). In London Dunne's new publisher, Robert H. Russell, arranged British syndication of the Dooley essays. Here, also, Ellis writes, "Dunne found himself lionized only slightly less than in New York, as Mr. Dooley's fame was bright in both England and Ireland" (*America,* 126). Among the celebrities he met were Charles Frohman, Ethel Barrymore, Anthony Hope Hawkins, James M. Barrie, and Mark Twain (*America,* 126).

Ethel Barrymore became the godmother of Finley Peter Dunne's second son, Philip; and Mark Twain became a friend for the ten years remaining of his life. In December 1935, Dunne wrote for his memoirs an essay commemorating Mark Twain at the centenary of his birth, remarking, "I didn't know Mark Twain as well as H. H. Rogers did, or William Dean Howells or Thomas Bailey Aldrich or that glorious Irishman Robert Collier, whom he fairly adored. But I saw a good deal of him" (*Remembers,* 241). Once Dunne received a summons from Mark Twain, who demanded, "Can't you write a Dooley about — — — — Lawson and the — — — — publisher of that — — — — magazine? . . . I have written thousands of words but I am always just cussing. If I could keep my faculty for humor uppermost I'd laugh the dogs out of the country. But I can't. I'm too mad" (*Remembers,* 260). Thomas W. Lawson was writing for *Everybody's* and attacking, among others, Henry H. Rogers of Standard Oil of New Jersey, who had helped Twain through the financial crisis following the bankruptcy of the publishing firm Webster and Company. Dunne could not defend anyone of "the Standard Oil crowd" but he did go on to satirize the muckrakers and, as Ellis writes, "made fun of the tendency to despair of democracy" (*America,* 213). Perhaps the keenest insight into Twain's perception of Dunne comes through in a comment that Dunne "is blessed beyond reason with friends" (*Remembers,* 267). For an accounting of those friends and of what friendship meant to Finley Peter Dunne, the "Commentary" by Philip Dunne serves as an adequate guide (*Remembers*, 211–38).

While in London, Dunne wrote some of the essays of the Molly Donahue series, made two excursions to Paris to visit Mary Abbott and her daughter Margaret; he wrote the five Dreyfus articles for syndication and for his third book, though without visiting the trial and using his old tactic of writing from newspaper accounts. He did visit Ireland—Dublin, Cork, and the counties of Queens and Kilkenny; that Mr. Dooley's Irishness was a literary device and lacked further commitment on the part of its Irish-American author seems borne out by the fact that Dunne did not visit Roscommon. He returned to work at the *Journal* on October 1; similarly, with Mr. Dooley's European excursion cut short, the location of the essays returned to the old Dooley haunts on Archey Road, of which Mr. Dooley remarked, "I'd rather be Dooley iv Chicago than th' Earl iv Peltville" (*America*, 132; *Philosophy*, 19–26).

But Grant Richards was not the only pirate in Dunne's life; a second work, called *What Dooley Says*, appeared in England with Dunne's name nowhere in evidence and was published in Chicago by Kazmar and Company, who did give credit to the *Chicago Evening Post*, whose clippings were the book's sources. The suit was settled without trial, but only when almost 15,000 copies had already been sold. In the meantime, Dunne's second book, *Mr. Dooley in the Hearts of His Countrymen* (1899), also reached the bestseller lists. In the judgment of Elmer Ellis, this book, with some of the pieces in it five years old, was the better of the two published thus far. Ellis writes that "it contained Dunne's finest tragic and didactic writing and the same high quality of satire and irony, gusty humor, and penetrating comment on public affairs as had characterized the better-known essays" (*America*, 135). Ellis notes, however, Dunne's careful editing of the selections: "Not one of the vigorous attacks on Powers, Pullman, or Yerkes . . . was ever published in one of his books, not because any of them were untrue, but simply because his kindliness forbade it" (*America*, 137). (These essays have been retrieved by Barbara C. Schaaf in her *Mr. Dooley's Chicago*, 1977.)

Dunne now drew upon public affairs extensively for his current writing but kept Dooley in character as an Irish saloon keeper. In November 1899 he wrote one of the most famous essays, a review of Theodore Roosevelt's *Rough Riders* (1899). His memoirs tell about the results of this essay, which actually began his acquaintance with Roosevelt, even though it satirized Roosevelt's egotism in making himself appear to have won the Spanish-American War single-handedly. Roosevelt wrote a letter inviting Dunne to visit him; but Dunne merely continued doing his *Journal* work and writing more Dooley essays, taking a trip to the West Coast, and returning to cover the national conventions—at which time his meeting with Roosevelt finally took place.

Dunne was now editor-in-chief of the *Chicago Journal* and, as he said, gave himself the assignment of covering the Republican convention. While there he received a message that Roosevelt wanted to see him, and bluntly foregoing all preliminaries Dunne asked whether the New York governor would accept the nomination for vice-president. On receiving an affirmative reply, Dunne writes, "I had only five minutes to get to the telegraph office and send a flash to my paper. It was the second and last scoop of my journalistic career" (*Remembers*, 189).

II   *National Attention*

The Roosevelt essay, simply titled "A Book Review," earned first position in the third collection, *Mr. Dooley's Philosophy* (1900); but before its appearance in the autumn, Dunne for a complex of reasons had moved from Chicago to New York. The third book registered smaller sales than the first two, possibly because of the public's overexposure to the Dooley essays, which were still being widely reprinted; and the book appeared only once on the bestseller list. At this time also, Dunne gave up writing a play he had been working on. Returning to Chicago briefly for Christmas, he remained two months suffering with typhoid fever and eventually, in February, took a trip to the Mediterranean. Upon his return in the spring he resumed writing the essays for *Harper's Weekly* and for newspapers on a variety of topics, and spent the summer of 1901 on Long Island with Robert Russell.

His essays on Booker T. Washington as a guest at the White House and on the Supreme Court were among those which became most famous. Concern for the plight of the black man led

Dunne to gauge Roosevelt's political success in terms of Washington's visit: "Well, annyhow, it's goin' to be th' roonation iv Prisidint Tiddy's chances in th' South. Thousan's iv men who wudden't have voted f'r him undher anny circumstances has declared that undher no circumstances wud they now vote f'r him." The combined pathos and insight of the conclusion show why Dunne through Mr. Dooley endeared himself to millions, even when they did not necessarily share his viewpoint. He concludes "The Booker Washington Incident" with Mr. Dooley saying, "I'd take away his right to vote an' his right to ate at th' same table an' his right to ride on th' cars an' even his sacred right to wurruk. I'd take thim all away an' give him th' on'y right he needs nowadays in th' South." When the ever-faithful Hennessy prompts him with the query, "What's that?" Dooley replies, "Th' right to live. If he cud start with that he might make something iv himsilf" (*Opinions,* 207-12). The other famous essay concluded with his oft-quoted remark on the Court, "No matther whether th' constitution follows th' flag or not, th' Supreme Court follows th' illiction returns." The essays from this year comprised the fourth book *Mr. Dooley's Opinions* (1901).

Dunne traveled to Mexico that year, and the following year visited London, Paris, Florence, and Rome, where he was invited to two audiences with Pope Leo XIII, the second one as part of a small group. In Paris he proposed to Margaret Abbott. He wrote editorials for *Collier's Weekly* and continued writing the Dooley essays on a variety of topics, including Sherlock Holmes, but mainly about American politics. These essays he collected in his fifth book, *Observations of Mr. Dooley* (1902); and, before his marriage to Margaret Abbott on December 9, he wrote for *Collier's Weekly* a Dooley piece on women in which the elderly bachelor "Guesses About Women" (see *America,* 180; *Philosophy,* 235-40).

Dunne's fame at this time was being expanded not only through the newspapers but also in magazines, among which Ellis lists *Harper's Weekly, Collier's, Century, Cosmopolitan, Ladies' Home Journal,* and the *Literary Digest* (*America,* 181) as publishing Dooley pieces. A popular song, the "Mr. Dooley March," was published in 1901; and in 1902 the song "Mister Dooley" by Jean Schwartz and William Jerome was first sung in a musical comedy called *The Chinese Honeymoon,* with Finley Peter Dunne, lured there by his friend William C. Whitney, in the audience.[5] The spotlight turned on the embarrassed Dunne as a popular singer sang, and the song became an instant success. Far away in Europe, some years later, it inspired a parody by James Joyce called "Dooleysprudence" (1916).

Also in 1902 Dunne accepted his friend William C. Whitney's offer to become editor for the *New York Morning Telegraph,* a paper which Whitney had acquired. When Whitney died in February of 1904, Dunne settled his interest in the paper for $30,000 and did not again find employment with a newspaper. The McClure Syndicate after 1904 paid Dunne $1,000 for each essay, but Dunne encountered increasing problems with meeting his own high standards, and his production was highly sporadic. He had never found writing his essays easy, even in the early days dashing them off at newspaper deadline; and now ten years of writing began to show their effect in difficulty with finding new themes and avoiding repetition. As Philip Dunne commented, "he might produce a good piece twice in a year, but not twice a week as in his early days" (*Remembers,* 163).

As Dunne's home life became steady, he and his family spent the winters in New York City and the summers at resorts. His son Finley Peter, Jr., was born in 1903, his son Philip in 1908, and the twins Margaret and Leonard in 1910. The friends of the elder Dunnes included Walter Damrosch and Benjamin Guinness among businessmen, writers, and entertainers. Perhaps Philip Dunne best provides an indication of how well the Dunnes lived when he speaks of his father as having "the tastes of a Morgan or a Rockefeller." Of his mother, Philip Dunne writes, "She honestly believed that to get along with less than four servants was a form of roughing it. And why not, when her friends had five or seven or even twenty?" (*Remembers,* 176). He recalls "spending the winters in a New England boarding school and the summers on Long Island" (*Remembers,* 171). Edith Wharton in *A Backward Glance* told about Dunne's meeting with Henry James (see *America,* 200). Along with his family life, Dunne continued his club life; and Elmer Ellis preserves a poem written by Michael Monahan, "To Finley Peter Dunne," extolling his "teaching a sad world how to smile," printed in *Papyrus* (February 1908).

Part of Dunne's essays had responded to efforts of the muckrakers, among whom in 1906 Ida Tarbell, Ray Stannard Baker, and Lincoln Steffens asked Dunne and William Allen

White to join them as editors and owners of the new *American Magazine* (see Ellis, 221–22). At the same time, his dialect pieces since 1902 were assembled by Harper's into the sixth book, *Dissertations by Mr. Dooley;* and Harper's also reissued the earlier books in a matched set (1906).

Dunne stayed with the *American* from 1906 to 1913, writing occasional dialect essays and an editorial each month and performing other editorial duties. His editorials belonged to the section of the magazine called "In the Interpreter's House," for which he created ongoing symbolic characters such as the Poet, the Philosopher, the Cynic, the Reporter, the Observer, and an especially satiric Mr. Worldly Wiseman to revive that of *Pilgrim's Progress.* The newspaper syndicate also received Dooley articles at this time. In addition, in 1911 Dunne wrote monthly articles for his friend Harry Payne Whitney's *Metropolitan* magazine for a period of six months, for a section called "From the Bleachers." Though he left his editorial position with the *American* in 1913, he continued writing for "In the Interpreter's House" until 1915, when Crowell Publishing bought the magazine.

Dunne's Dooley essays after 1905 featured the life-insurance scandals and prominent persons such as Andrew Carnegie, John D. Rockefeller, and Theodore Roosevelt. The Hague Conference became an obvious target for satire because of its failure to accomplish anything. The new Dooley essays up to 1910 appeared in book form in *Mr. Dooley Says* (1910), brought out by Charles Scribner's Sons and containing twenty-one long pieces. "Perhaps the best political satire Dunne ever wrote," Ellis believes, was in this collection, that on the Payne-Aldrich tariff (*America,* 247); but public response was disheartening enough that Dunne and his publishers canceled a sequel projected for 1911.

After Dunne left the editorial position with the *American* in 1913, he joined *Collier's Weekly* in a similar capacity, and by 1915 had a page of his own for which he and others wrote under the titles "Comment on Politics" and "Comment on Congress." Dunne found the war very depressing, and there were no Dooley essays from 1915 to 1919. In 1919 he brought out the eighth and last book of Dooley essays, *Mr. Dooley on Making a Will and Other Necessary Evils;* it contains nineteen essays, with all but two written before 1915. Its sales and public response, however, were better than those for the previous book.

Briefly in 1917 Dunne edited the *Pioneer Bulletin* and headed the War Savings Stamp campaign in New York City. In the fall of 1917, after Mark Sullivan died, Dunne took over as chief editor of *Collier's*; but Robert Collier died just as the war ended, leaving his share of *Collier's* to Dunne, Harry Payne Whitney, and Francis P. Garvan. Philip Dunne in his commentary in the *Memoirs* tells the story of the three friends' renunciation of this legacy in order to aid Mrs. Collier (*Remembers,* 221); but Dunne's editorship came to an end later in 1919 when Mrs. Collier sold the magazine to Crowell Publishing Company.

During this time Dunne was instrumental in the development of the National Golf Links of America course at Southampton, Long Island; and the family began spending summers at Southampton. He supported Warren G. Harding for the presidency in 1920 and played golf with him. He suffered long illness and two operations in 1923, but in 1924 successfully revived the Mr. Dooley essays for the Bell Syndicate by selecting and shortening old Dooley articles; these ran for two years. He was guest of honor for the Harvest Home Dinner at the National Golf Links in 1925 at which Lancy Nicoll read a special poetic tribute to Dunne (most of which Elmer Ellis quotes — *America,* 276-77). In 1926 Dunne began a weekly series of new Dooley essays for the magazine *Liberty,* and these continued for twenty issues from February into July 1926.

Frequently during his career with the Dooley essays, Dunne had been fortunate in and honored by the illustrators of the essays. Especially his third book, *Mr. Dooley's Philosophy* (1900) had been touched by the artful genius of illustrators E. W. Kemble, William Nicholson, and F. B. Opper. Dunne himself had been honored to be one of only two Americans (the other was Mark Twain) drawn by the British cartoonist "Spy," the caricaturist whose real name was Sir Leslie Ward (1851-1922); it was his "portrait" of Dunne which was said by friends to be the best picture of Dunne and which Elmer Ellis used for a frontispiece for his *Mr. Dooley's America.* Now, for *Liberty* magazine, the illustrations were superb and presented Mr. Dooley and his topics at their lively best as imagined by Albert T. Reid, R. B. Fuller, and most consistently once more, E. W. Kemble.

In very few of the collected essays did Dunne concern himself with the businesses he and his Mr. Dooley conducted, namely bartending and journalism. In "The Bar," he discusses seriously whether liquor is a vice, a necessity, or an evil. Mr. Dooley says, "Liquor is not a nicissry evil. Hogan says it's wan way iv ra-alizin' th' ideel. Th' nex' day ye'er ashamed iv ye're ideel. Th' throuble about it is that whin ye take it ye want more. But that's the throuble with ivrything ye take." Everything includes power and money. When drink became a political issue amid agitation for the Prohibition Amendment (passed by Congress in December 1917), Dooley observed the change in sentiment from that of his younger days: "A statesman wud no more be seen goin' into a saloon thin he wud into a meetin' iv th' Anti-Semitic league," he said in his last anthology. The Twenty-First Amendment, passed by Congress and ratified in 1933, repealed the Eighteenth; during those days of prohibition, Dunne let Mr. Dooley speak out on his outlawed profession. He acknowledges less overhead, now that all he needs is "A modest little back room, a closet, a bottle iv household ammonya, an' a fri'nd in th' revnoo foorce." He sees his customers divided on the burning question of the day, whether prohibition is a failure—depending on which are willing to risk becoming outlaws by buying a drink—and he wishes the question would be soon reduced to ashes. Doc Larkin, however, prospers with his stomach-pumping business, as does the undertaker when the stomach pump does not arrive in time; and the ingredients of bootleg whiskey include the contents of the fire extinguisher, furniture polish, by-products of the lumber yard, and formaldehyde. The navy prospers with attempting to run down rum runners. But Mr. Dooley remains neutral; he admits only that "I wudd'nt care if there wasn't a dhrop iv it in th' wurruld ontil somebody told me I cudd'nt have it an' thin i'd use it on'y be th' bucket" (*Liberty*, April 17, 1926).

More frequently Dunne referred to the antics of journalists and to their profession. In "Christian Journalism," Dooley tells about a Kansas man who determined to start a moral newspaper so that immoral news would not corrupt the nation. Dooley delights in listing the obnoxious and pallid contents of such a paper, and finds that even Father Kelly confesses, "They ain't anny news in bein' good." When Father Kelly searches the papers to find the news about the murder and burglary set, Dooley knows why people do not go to church. Regarding "An Editor's Duties," he said, "They'se nawthin' so hard as mindin' ye'er own business an' an iditor niver has to do that." In "The News of the Week," Mr. Dooley gives an encyclopedic summary of the world's events, but Mr. Hennessy wants to know whether anyone has not been killed. Dooley disagrees that newspapers have to print what happens; he says they have to print what is different. In "Newspaper Publicity," he tackles the problem of journalists in their law-enforcement activities, exposing evil and corruption, so that wrongdoers seem to be "hauled off in th' circylation wagon to th' newspaper office" where they are tried and convicted by the press; also he considers what amounts to invasion of privacy, with complete coverage of the individual throughout his life. Dooley says, "We march through life an' behind us marches th' phottygrafter an' th' rayporther. There are no such things as private citizens."

Without giving the source for the essay, Edward J. Bander in *Mr. Dooley in the Court of Law* (1963) reproduces another Dunne essay in which Mr. Dooley says, "Th' hand that rocks th' fountain pen is th' hand that rules th' wurruld."[6] It seems a fitting conclusion to the power of the written word, to which Dunne devoted his life.

III *Retirement*

Between 1915 and 1926 the hiatus in Dunne's output disappointed many people, although he had certainly earned his laurels and deserved a rest. On the dwindling of his father's literary output in these later years, Philip Dunne cites recurring illness and explains further, "To some extent, the prodigal outpourings of his youth had exhausted him. He had run out of appropriate subjects. Finally, in his later years, the world itself moved out of the purview of the humorist. As he said in one of these essays, insanity and racial murder are not fit subjects for humor. And yet a revived Mr. Dooley could not have pretended that such things didn't exist" (*Remembers*, 226-27). When Dunne wrote at this time he wrote out of economic necessity; but the essays in *Liberty* magazine in 1926 show no lag in quality. In 1927, however, Payne Whitney died, leaving Dunne and two of his friends half a million dollars each (see *Remembers*, 177, 226).

What happened to the fortune has been variously discussed, but apparently there is no mystery about it. Dunne had always loved luxury and had spent heavily; such activities as enjoying the winter and spring of 1928 and 1929 with his wife in Palm Beach could not have been economic living. Also, he lost some money in the stock-market crash of 1929. In these last years, continuing his activities in golf clubs and other men's clubs, he became, according to Elmer Ellis, "Mr. Dooley incarnate"—a celebrity and warm friend welcomed in many circles. Philip Dunne, in those last years with his father, came to know, as he wrote, "why rulers of nations had maneuvered for his friendship, why intellectuals from Henry Adams to Felix Frankfurter had respected him on their own terms. It was not for his wit nor his charm nor his political acumen, but for the quality of his mind. It was sheer intellect which had carried him to the top of his world. The chief characteristic of his mind was total clarity. He saw through the flesh to the skeleton of things" (*Remembers,* 180).

Ill health, however, became publicly obvious when Dunne could not, in 1933, attend an anniversary press function at the World's Fair in Chicago, forty years after the World's Columbian Exposition which had been the subject of his early Colonel McNeery pieces. A throat ailment in 1934 preceded a 1935 diagnosis of cancer, and Dunne, at his son Philip's urging, wrote the memoirs while taking treatments.

Dunne had, as everyone must, faced the problem of approaching death. In his essay "The End of Things," Mr. Dooley had indulged in the fantasy of the dead hearing words of praise spoken above and around his corpse; but Mr. Dooley—a realist always—knew in his soul that the conversation, instead of extolling his virtues, would consist of idle remarks such as "It's a nice day f'r a dhrive to th' cimitry. Did he lave much?"

In the example of Finley Peter Dunne, the fantasy was close to the reality. Philip tells the story of his father's death at the age of sixty-nine and a magnificent funeral (*Remembers,* 13, 15); the death occurred after brief optimism about treatment of the cancer was rudely shattered by a hemorrhage in the throat. Dunne had desired a simple funeral, but adoring friends and public made it one of the largest in St. Patrick's Cathedral in New York City. A memorial Mass was celebrated in St. Bridget's Church on Archey Avenue.

CHAPTER 2

Is He Irish at All?

THE Irish settling in Chicago in the nineteenth century established themselves along "Archey Road" or Archer Avenue, where Dunne later visualized the pub of Mr. Dooley, an Irish-American nonagenarian of remarkable memory and astuteness, and settled into it as listener its most enduring customer, another Irish-American, only eighty years old, named Mr. Hennessy. To many people, both Dunne and Mr. Dooley were without doubt Irish-American. Others, among whom is Philip Dunne, disagree; responding to a proposed discussion topic, he wrote early in 1978,

I have to say frankly that I dislike "The Irishness of Mr. Dooley." The country seems to have gone on a binge of ethnicity, but Mr. D's identity as an Irishman was the *least* important of his attributes (see F. P. D.'s chapter "On the Irish" in *Mr. Dooley Remembers* and my own introduction to it). I appeared on a panel last year on the Los Angeles public television station and was horrified to hear the announcer introduce the subject as "the ethnic humorist, Finley Peter Dunne." My father's choice of an Irishman as his mouthpiece to express his own political analyses was entirely incidental. Aside from a few "Irish" pieces, especially in the early days, he spoke always as an American, dealing with American and world issues. Eliminate the brogue and the pieces stand out as what they were: pure Americana.

I had this brought home to me in a delightful way a few years ago when the Friends of the Library at the University of Southern California put on "An Evening with Mr. Dooley." I got Arthur Schlesinger to do the historical background and, on the urging of my friend Page Smith, then Provost of Cowell College, U. C. Santa Cruz, Peter Beagle, author of *The Last Unicorn,* to join with me in reading excerpts from the Dooley pieces. Peter is an avid Dooley fan: where I have to read the material, he can quote entire pages from memory. I told him that I didn't plan to attempt a brogue (though in truth I'm better at it than F. P. D. himself, whose accent was pure Chicago!), and

Peter replied that he *would* use the brogue, because that was half the fun. Well, Peter's "brogue" came straight out of "Fiddler on the Roof." And the astonishing thing is that it took nothing whatever away from Mr. Dooley. Done in pure Irish brogue, Yiddish, or my own rather Harvard English, it matters not one whit: it is still Mr. Dooley. It is the *content* that counts, not the manner of its presentation.

I correspond with many Dooley fans, and surprisingly few of them are Irish. Some are Jews, some proper Bostonians, some Englishmen—there is no *ethnic* common denominator. . . . I am proud of the half of my blood that is Irish, but far prouder of my father's place as a mover and shaker in a purely American tradition.[1]

I   *Ireland in Chicago and Abroad*

For his memoirs, in the chapter "On the Irish," Finley Peter Dunne looked back over forty some years and summed up his attitude this way:

My father was only six years old when he was brought to New Brunswick by his parents, and remembered absolutely nothing about the old country. In all my life I have spent only a fortnight there. True it was a delightful fortnight, but it wasn't long enough to root me to the soil. I don't believe all Irishmen are honest, loyal, capable, kind, humorous, brave and musical. But let no Englishmen tell me they're not. My languid pulses respond at once to a tale of the suffering of Ireland under British rule. I'm moved, too, but not so much, by the suffering of Ireland under Irish rule. It was no Englishman who murdered Michael Collins. (*Remembers*, 32)

The few Irish pieces Philip Dunne referred to include those which actually spoke satirically against the Irish. The essay "On the Anglo-Saxon," for example, employed the familiar device of ridicule-by-flattery and satire of mass mania. As a man behind the guns—"four thousan' miles behind thim, an' willin' to be further"—Dooley saw clearly that he and Hogan must bring about the proposed Anglo-Saxon alliance of 1898 single-handedly, and that such an alliance would surely crush the Spanish and bring security to the world. "An Anglo-Saxon, Hinnissy," he explains, "is a German that's forgot who was his parents." Then he proceeds to name people of various nationalities who see their advantage in aligning themselves with England. In Chicago itself, "We've got together an Anglo-Saxon 'lieance in this wa-ard, an' we're goin' to ilict Sarsfield O'Brien prisidint, Robert Immitt Clancy sicrety, an' Wolfe Tone Malone three-asurer. O'Brien'll be a good wan to have. He was in the Fenian r-raid, an' his father carrid a pike in forty-eight. An' he's in th' Clan. Besides, he has a sthrong pull with th' Ancient Ordher iv Anglo-Saxon Hibernyans" (*Peace*, 53-57).

To cement that alliance Lord Charles Beresford (1846-1919) came to the United States as, said Mr. Dooley, "a sort iv advance agent iv th' White Man's Burden Thrajeedy Company" and a message that the untamed American cousins who speak English must be taught English manners. Mr. Dooley estimates the character of Lord Beresford as that of "two little Evas, four hundherd millyon Topsies, six hundherd millyon Uncle Toms." With remarkable clairvoyance, Dooley foresaw that the Irish would side with Germany to obtain their own freedom from Britain, as they planned roughly sixteen years later: "If th' 'liance got into a war with Garmany, an' some wan was to start a rough-an'-tumble in Ireland abut iliction time, I wondher wud th' ciment hold!" (*Hearts*, 18-22).

Dooley insisted that England, while advocating the peaceful behavior of the gentleman of honor, would not respect anything except force. By 1906 Arthur James Balfour (1848-1930) had passed from being England's prime minister (1902-1905) to being Unionist leader of opposition and had refused as Speaker in the House of Commons a discussion of the Irish question as requested by Frank Hugh O'Donnell, the Home Rule politician. O'Donnell had earlier written that "the tactlessness of Englishmen, of men of high order, is the most difficult of the difficulties of the Empire"[2] and now had no choice but to walk out of the House. Dooley explains, "Ye can't be a rivolutionist in a silk hat an' a long coat. Riv'lution is wurruk f'r th' shirtsleeves. A riv'lution can't be bound be th' rules iv th' game because it's again' th' rules iv th' game." He deplores the fact that the English don't understand Irish, though they do understand German, Turk, Chinese, and Indian, and concludes with an insight proper to the North Irish question after 1968: "England will niver free Ireland, but some day, if we make it inthrestin' enough f'r her she'll have to free England iv Ireland. An' that'll be all right" (*Dissertations*, 129-34).

Continuing his satire of Americans' eagerness to identify with England, Dunne pronounced Theodore Roosevelt's presidential election in 1904 an "Anglo-Saxon Triumph." Among European dignitaries celebrating the victory, the British were foremost: "On hearin' th' glad news on th' Saturdah followin' th' iliction, th' king sint f'r Ambassadure Choate, who came as fast as his hands an' knees wud carry him." Roosevelt was elected with the assistance of the Clan na Gael, which is "wan iv th' sthrongest Anglo-Saxon organyzations we have. It's whole purpose is to improve Anglo-Saxon civilyzation be ilivatin' it." The support of "Casey" and the Irish-American football players as potential soldiers amount in Dooley's logic to a foregone conclusion: "Prisidint Hadley [of Yale] or Prisidint Eliot [of Harvard] makes an addhress at th' king's birthday dinner, an' rejoices in our inthrest in Anglo-Saxon spoorts, an' congratylates th' wurruld that hereafther if England has a war we will have a chance to do most iv th' fightin' an' pay half th' money" (*Dissertations,* 213–18).

The broad outlines of the Irish-content essays expose, then, basic Irish national issues: the contention with England (often reversed or stood on end for purposes of satire); the dissension between the Orange men of the Protestant North and the devotees of green in the Catholic South; the doings of heroes such as Robert Emmett (1778–1803), Charles Parnell (1846–1891), Patrick Sarsfield (d. 1693), and Wolfe Tone (1763–1798); and Irish events such as the Phoenix Park murders of Lord Frederick Cavendish and his Undersecretary Burke (1882). Sarsfield, hero of the losing side in the Battle of the Boyne in 1690 (still celebrated in North Ireland each year on July 12), earns Dooley's admiration. In "Boyne Water and Bad Blood," Dooley describes an Orange parade in Chicago to commemorate the victory of the Protestant forces of William of Orange (1650–1702) over the Catholic forces of James II (1633–1701): "Whin th' twelfth day iv July come around an' th' Orangeys got ready to cillybrate th' day King Willum, with al his Gatlin' guns an' cannon, just barely sthud off Sarsfield an' his men that had on'y pikes an' brickbats an' billyard cues." He muses over the idea of a St. Patrick's Day celebrated on the twelfth of July, and admits that he would not raise a hand against an Orangeman, "though me cousin Tim was kilt be wan iv thim dhroppin' a bolt on his skull in th' ship-yards in Belfast. 'T'was lucky f'r that there Orangey he spoke first. Me cousin Tim had a ship-ax in his hand that'd 've evened things up f'r at laste wan iv

th' poor pikemen that Sarsfield had along with him." The
Chicago Orange parade was well regulated by ranks of police
until one Irish-American shouted "Th' 'ell with King Willum"
and an Orange man answered, "Th' 'ell with th' pope." Then
came the free-for-all (*Hearts,* 85–91).

In the preface to his first book, Dunne described the Irish
community of "Archey Road," a place where "you can hear all
the various accents of Ireland . . . you can see the wakes and
christenings, the marriages and funerals, and the other fetes of
the ol' counthry somewhat modified and darkened by American
usage. The Banshee has been heard many times in Archey Road.
On the eve of All Saints' Day it is well known that here alone the
pookies play thricks in cabbage gardens. In 1893 it was reported
that Malachi Dempsey was called 'by the other people,' and
disappeared west of the tracks, and never came back" (*Peace,*
viii–ix). But several of the most successful of the Chicago essays
properly speak to wider nonethnic audiences.

Dunne's essay "On Criminals," one of those memorized and
recited for various gatherings, demonstrates his talent for writing
serious drama and tells the story of Petey Scanlan, whose mother
came from County Kerry and who "growed up fr'm bein' a curly-
haired angel f'r to be th' toughest villyun in th' r-road." With the
police afraid to capture the criminal amid a street filled with
patrol wagons and a suggestion that they set fire to the house,
"Thin th' fr-ront dure opened, an' who shud come out but th'
little mother." On hearing an explanation of the problem, the
mother turned back into the house: " 'T'was less than a minyit
befure she come out, clingin' to th' la-ad's ar'rm. 'He'll go,' she
says. 'Thanks be, though he's wild, they'se no crime on his head.
Is there, dear?' " The lad manages a noble lie and departs in
police custody. The ending of the essay recalls William Butler
Yeats's poem "The Ballad of Father Gilligan" and his proof that a
god "With planets in his care, / Has pity on the least of things."
The father returns home to find the mother peacefully dead,
"settin' in a big chair with her apron in her hands an' th' picture
iv th' la-ad in her lap" (*Peace,* 124–29).

In another serious essay titled "Shaughnessy," Dunne dis-
paraged the Irish-Catholic tradition that one son of each
household must become a priest: " 'Tis a poor fam'ly that hasn't
some wan that's bein' iddycated f'r th' priesthood while all th'
rest wear thimsilves to skeletons f'r him, an' call him Father Jawn

'r Father Mike whin he comes home wanst a year, light-hearted an' free, to eat with thim." Shaughnessy himself bears the death of the would-be priest son, then his daughter, another son, his wife, and the twins. The one remaining daughter leaves him alone when she marries; and the essay closes with the poignant image of sorrow of an old man who had borne six deaths with fortitude now reduced to utter loneliness, "with his elbows on his knees an' th' empty pipe between his teeth" (*Hearts*, 45–49).

The Irish spirit of nationality Dooley found expressed somewhat violently in games such as knock-the-baby-down and the shooting gallery at picnics, all of which he discussed in "The Freedom Picnic." "Be hivins," he says, "if Ireland cud be freed be a picnic, it'd not on'y be free to-day, but an impire, begorra." The redeeming fact, he claims, is that picnics are less harmful than blowing up Westminster Cathedral: "'Tis a dam sight asier thin goin' over with a slug iv joynt powder an blowin' up a polis station with no wan in it. It costs less; an', whin 'tis done, a man can lep aboord a sthreet ca-ar, an' come to his family an' sleep it off." For himself, when he attends the picnic, Dooley says, "I suppose I must've freed as much as eight counties in Ireland" (*Hearts*, 92–95).

"The O'Briens Forever" satirizes a political convention at which both nominators and nominees are more willing to fight than speak. Hennessy with great Irish devotion writes a biography of the candidate, Chicago alderman William J. O'Brien, and sets forth all the Irish stereotypes: poverty, fights, poor education, boxing championship, political career, fights, and a heart that beats "up close to th' ribs iv th' common people." With great indignation Mr. Dooley informs him that it was not "our" Bill O'Brien who was nominated for president but a Nebraska man (William Jennings Bryan). Hennessy protests, "I seen him on th' flure. He had th' sinitor iv Missoury be th' throat whin ye took me away." Knowing that all Irish are related in spirit if not in blood, Hennessy, undeterred, continues his "novel" with the intention of making it "a sketch iv th' cousin iv th' candydate" (*Hearts*, 101–106). With modest understatement, Georg Mann in "Call for Mr. Dooley" has observed, "Dunne was probably guilty of encouraging the myth of Irish belligerence for the amusement of his readers."[3]

"The Quick and the Dead" continues the fighting theme and extends it. Based on an incident similar to that of "The Ballad of

Tim Finnegan" which inspired James Joyce's novel *Finnegans Wake* (1939), this essay tells the story of O'Grady, who fell from a scaffold, then as "ghost" rose from the dead to visit his widow and her new husband. As Dooley tells the story, the husband decides to deal with the ghost by accusing him of failing to pay the rent and of insulting the dead with his earthly prowling. With this the new husband and O'Grady "clinched an' rowled on th' flure." This risen ghost also can commit murder, for both the ex-wife and the new husband are soon found dead. As for fighting other ghosts, Dooley concludes, "in a round an' tumble fight he cud lick a St. Patrick's Day procession iv thim" (*Hearts,* 190-95).

In "The Irishman Abroad," Dooley returns to a familiar theme and utters his highest praise of the Irish. Recalling something of the content of the Anglo-Saxon essays, Dooley says, "our people makes poor Irishmen, but good Dutchmen . . . th' rale boney fide Irishman is no more thin a foreigner born away from home." Inspired by a newspaper article about Count Eduard von Taaffe (1833-1895), Austrian premier of Irish descent, Dooley recalls Robert Dwyer Joyce's poem about "Taaffe in Austhria." Of the Irish as a whole, he says, "Whin there's battles to be won, who do they sind for? McMahon or Shurdan or Phil Kearney or Colonel Colby. Whin there's books to be wrote, who writes thim but Char-les Lever or Oliver Goldsmith or Willum Carleton? Whin there's speeches to be made, who makes thim but Edmund Burke or Macchew P. Brady? There's not a land on th' face iv th' wurruld but th' wan where an Irishman doesn't stand with his fellow-man, or above thim. . . . There's Mac's an' O's in ivry capital iv Europe atin' off silver plates whin their relations is staggerin' under th' creels iv turf in th' Connaught bogs." Dooley anticipates the obvious question from his listener, John McKenna: why don't the Irish do as much for their own country? Dooley builds his answer around a metaphor: "Ye can't grow flowers in a granite block, Jawn dear, much less whin th' first shoot'd be thrampled under foot without pity. . . there's no soil in Ireland f'r th' greatness iv th' race; an' there has been none since th' wild geese wint across th' say to France, hangin' like flies to th' side iv th' Fr-rinch ship" (*Hearts,* 202-205).

A disgruntled Mr. Dooley responds to Hennessy's question about St. Patrick's Day, "Oh, ye mane th' day th' low Irish that hasn't anny votes cillybrates th' birth iv their naytional saint, who was a Fr-rinchman." That votes can be bought and that interests

turn becomes the subject of "The Decline of National Feeling."
Chief among turncoats is President McKinley, who "was fr'm th'
north iv Ireland two years ago, an' not so far north ayether,—just
far enough north f'r to be on good terms with Derry an' not far
enough to be bad frinds with Limerick. He was raised on
butthermilk an' haggis, an' he dhrank his Irish nate with a dash iv
orange bitthers in it. He's been movin' steadily north since; an', if
he keeps on movin', he'll go r-round th' globe, an' bring up
somewhere in th' south iv England." Among others Dooley
pronounces "Hinnery Cabin Lodge" the second most famous
lapsed Irishman, a bould Fenian who has "changed his chune, an'
'tis 'Sthrangers wanst, but brothers now,' with him, an' 'Hands
acrost th' sea an' into some wan's pocket' " (*Hearts*, 222–27).

II *Dooley Replaces McNeery*

The first essay Dunne titled "St. Patrick's Day" was published
March 21, 1896, some years after the celebration had been
established as the greatest Irish-American holiday in Chicago.
Dooley now is entirely done in by the events and the changes,
feeling that old age has well caught up with him: "If I was to take
count of th' minyits be how I feel afther Pathrick's day I'd be too
old to do annything with but print in th' Inter Ocean." The chief
complaint and sorrow stem from the changing of the parade
route to Michigan Avenue, where "There ain't a vote or a
subscriber to th' Citizen there an' they'se twinty-sivin blocks iv
unfrindly houses without enough dhrink to start a fight on." The
"joods" dressed up to march in the parade evoke his deepest
scorn: "now it might as well be th' annivarsary iv th' openin' iv th'
first clothin' store in Chicago."[4]
One of Dunne's best statements on the Irish and on Irish-
Americans begins with a pugilistic-nostalgic discussion between
John McKenna and a policeman on the occasion of Colonel
McNeery's return to Ireland in an essay intended as the formal
announcement on Dunne's part that McNeery henceforth would
be out of the essays. McKenna says, "He was a most sarcastic
man, that there McNeery, an' no love had he f'r anny but thim
that come from th' same dirty little parish with him." McKenna
recovers from McNeery's departure by getting his Irish up in
celebration of Irish Day at the World's Columbian Exposition,
about which he promises and threatens at once: "We'll all be

there sittin' in peace an' concord, an' if iver a man says ill iv
Charles Stewart Parnell I'll poke him in th' eye if I die f'r it. No
Dutch need apply tomorrow."[5]

Whether a saloon is "typically Irish" remains to be debated;[6]
that the saloon was a popular resort in Dooley's day no one need
doubt. Barbara Schaaf in *Mr. Dooley's Chicago* (1977) writes that
"according to *Mixed Drinks: The Saloonkeepers Journal*, per
capita consumption in the city — even including children — was
forty-nine gallons per year in 1890. Thirsty Chicagoans and their
visitors consumed almost 3 million barrels of malt drinks during
the World's Fair year of 1893."[7] No wonder, then, that Mr.
Dooley found it difficult to maintain both his clientele and his
honesty. In "Mr. Dooley's Trials," he responds to the differing
opinions about the verdict in the Cronin murder trial and laments
that he had sworn off lying during Lent; he complains that "th'
minyit a man opens a little licker shtore, be dad, his opinion is as
valible as if he was th' dhriver iv a shtreetcar." To Schneider, the
Dutchman, Dooley says, "If 'twas wan iv ye'er people he'd be
hung." To Maloney he says, "Huroo. 'Tis a vindication iv us again
th' dips." To Hogan he says, "How cud they do it? 'Tis a
disgrace." In spite of Dooley's diplomacy, soon Maloney and
Hogan clash, and Dooley explains, "They'd 'iv massacreed each
other if it wasn't f'r me puttin' th' feet into Hogan an' callin' for a
German polisman." But the impossibility of being everyone's
friend now becomes evident. His listener, John McKenna,
accuses Dooley of being a member of "camp ninety-six," Dr.
Cronin's camp in the Clan na Gael.[8]

Mr. Dooley's "Christmas in Ireland" provides no glorious
cheer but rather paints a picture of poverty and simple
pleasures, such as the return of farflung sons, walking the length
of Ireland if necessary to be at home for Christmas. One
difference between an Irish and an American Christmas, Dooley
explains, is that the Irish had no "Sandy Clause." "Why is it, 'd'ye
suppose? I never knew that St. Patrick druv him out with th'
snakes, but I niver heerd iv him till I come to this counthry."
Christmas was the time the priests received their annual
contributions from the parish, a feature of Catholic life which
earns Dooley's satiric touch: "By gar, some iv thim soggarths was
bor-rn politicians, f'r they cud jolly a man f'r givin' big an' roast
him f'r givin' a little till ivry citizen in th' parish was thryin' to
bate his neighbor like as if 'twas at a game iv give-away. Ye'd

hear thim comin' home fr'm th' church. 'Th' iday iv Mike Casey givin' tin shillin's whin Badalia Casey burrid a pinch iv tay f'rm me on'y las' week.' "[9]

Irish sentiment in Chicago expressed itself politically in the Fenian invasion of Canada (chiefly 1886), in the formation of the Clan na Gael (1867), and in ward politics. Dunne wrote additional Irish-content essays which he did not collect in his first two books, intended as they were for national audiences. In *Mr. Dooley's Chicago,* Barbara Schaaf reprints, under the chapter heading "Mr. Dooley on the Immigrant Experience," several additional essays on Irish topics: "To Free Old Ireland," "Why Dooley Quit," "Dooley at the Fair," "Dooley in the Storm" on his crossing of the Atlantic, and untitled others on the Fenians, the black list, aid to the poor, on the poor, and on Bridgeport bridge traffic which should be guarded by an Irishman.[10] Charles Fanning in *Mr. Dooley and the Chicago Irish* (1976) entitles his corresponding chapter "Cathleen ni Houlihan in Chicago: Irish-American Nationalism" and adds to those essays already discussed "The Fenian Invasion of Canada," "The Venezuela Boundary and the Irish Republic," "The Dynamite Campaign in the Clan na Gael," "An Irish-German Alliance in Bridgeport," "The Flight of the Wild Geese," "Hypocritical Journalism: Jingoes and Nationalists," "Gladstone and Parnell," "The British Cabinet Crisis of 1895," and "The Tynan Plot."[11]

The Fenians had been organized as the American branch of the Irish Republican Brotherhood as far back as 1858; the Fenian invasion of Canada, intended to acquire seaboard territory from which Fenian privateers could capture English fleets, consisted from the start of the stuff of which comedy is made. The decisive battle occurred on June 2, 1886, when American volunteers clashed with Toronto college boys called "The Queen's Own." Malcolm Brown describes the engagement in few words: "After a three-hour battle in which six Fenians and twelve Canadians were killed, The Queen's Own fled, leaving the Fenians in possession of the field of battle. . . . By June 3, 1866, the foremost military problem of the hour had become the question of who would pay the railroad fares home for seven thousand stranded Fenian soldiers."[12] (The number may be disputed.) Dunne wrote the "Fenian Invasion of Canada" for his June 15, 1895, Dooley piece, recalling that his uncle Mike, a brigadier general, was one of "more gin'rals thin ye cud find in a

Raypublican West Town convintion." But among determined Irish-Americans armed with baseball bats and other assorted weapons, Mike soon wearied of British who refused to stand up and fight and returned to Buffalo, only to be arrested for "rivolution" (*Hearts,* 158–64).

In addition to his role in exposing the murderer of Dr. Cronin, Dunne knew, personally through his policeman friend John Shea, of the $10,000 raised by patriotic Irish-Americans to hire Chicagoan Patrick O'Donnell to kill James Carey, who needed to be punished for having participated in the Phoenix Park murders but who was free to travel the world at British government expense because he had turned Queen's evidence. Also, the British government had tried to implicate Parnell in the murders in order to discredit him. With Shea's assistance in recovering the money after O'Donnell lost it in gambling, O'Donnell succeeded in this political assassination. Dunne knew that Shea "hated crimes of violence," and regarding Shea's role commented, "It is impossible to understand this attitude of Shea, unless you appreciate the intense hatred of the British Government that the Irishman in every part of the world cherished in his heart" (*Remembers,* 67).

In his memoirs, Dunne tells about his acquaintance with Michael Collins (1890–1922), an Irishman he admired greatly, and the meeting with Winston Churchill at which Collins signed the Irish Free State treaty and, in his own words, his own death warrant. That the enemies of Ireland were its own people Dunne knew well, for his closing remarks on this incident allude to an Irish murderer of an Irishman: "Within a very few weeks this dauntless man was murdered from ambush near his birthplace in the county of Cork. His murderer is known and still lives"—an ironic contrast to the story of James Carey (see *Remembers,* 97–98).

In later years, Dunne writes in his memoirs, "Most of us lost interest in Irish affairs." But there came a brief revival with the visit of Lady Gregory and the Abbey Players in 1911 to perform John M. Synge's play *The Playboy of the Western World* in New York; and along with it came the determination of some Irish-Americans, led by Dunne's friend John Devoy, to stage a protest, as had the Irish in Dublin, against this "libel on Ireland." Dunne considered the play unworthy of the effort, but John Devoy was a capable newspaperman and editor of the *Gaelic American,* in which Dunne held some small stock. Lady Gregory he admired greatly, "as gentle and lovable and kind a person as I ever met" but also "every bit as Irish as any Devoy that ever came out of Kildare." Despite Dunne's attempts to escape the performance, he sat in Lady Gregory's box with Colonel Roosevelt and Colonel Robert Emmett through an evening of high comedy staged by the audience. With vegetables thrown at male performers and singing of rival songs by rival factions in the audience, Lady Gregory stood in her box and shouted at people to reserve their strength for a second performance, after the demonstration should end. Dunne saw that all happened as she urged, and "This very moderate comedy has the distinction of having been played twice in one night, or at least once and a half" (*Remembers*, 82–87).

Before Dunne left Chicago, however, he did not function as nonpartisan creator of Mr. Dooley without creating also some enemies. Chief among these was John Finerty, advocate of the dynamite campaign to blow up symbols of British nationalists; member of the Clan na Gael, which was founded to overthrow British rule; and founder of the *Citizen*, Chicago's Irish revolutionary newspaper. Dunne's essay "The Tynan Plot" made high comedy of a serious matter, chiefly through exaggeration of the publicity attendant upon an attempt of P. J. P. Tynan of New York to assassinate Queen Victoria and the visiting Czar by tunneling under Buckingham Palace and blowing it up, or, as Dooley phrased it, "he figured out that th' thrue way to free Ireland was to go over an' blow th' windows in Winzer Palace, an' incidentally to hist th' queen an' th' Rooshian cza-ar without th' aid iv th' elevator." Tynan was arrested in France in September 1896 but released when authorities discovered he had written a 700-page book "for the Dynamite Campaign and the murder of Lord Frederick Cavendish in Dublin's Phoenix Park."[13]

Not merely Dunne's savage comedy of Irish-American fiascoes, however, aroused the opposition of John Finerty. It was also Dunne's use of dialect, which Finerty, as Charles Fanning reports, "had long since come to resent. . . . He often complained in the *Citizen* about the use of 'the devil of dialectism' to degrade the Irish race." Fanning points to *Citizen* editorials written by Finerty advocating dynamite in the 1880s, the excesses of which "were hardly tempered in the otherwise quieter nineties. He continued to advocate terror bombing and physical force, 'the platform,' as he put it in 1894, 'of Tone, Emmet, Mitchel, and the Fenians.' When Gladstone died in 1897, Finerty dismissed him as 'politically, as rotten an agent, up to within a decade of his death, as ever lent his services to the accursed empire which he served so faithfully.' " When Dunne's preface to his first book (1898) announced the location of Martin Dooley's home territory as "forninst th' gas-house and beyant Healey's slough and not far from the polis station," Finerty published in the *Citizen* soon thereafter (April 1899) a doggerel poem called "Dooley's Lamentation" which repeats the location of the saloon "Not far from Healy's Slough."[14] Nor did Dunne's occasionally ribald treatment of the Clan na Gael earn him friends among its members.

III   An Afterview of "Irishness"

Dunne's Irish days were chiefly his Chicago days, before he became widely famous and moved to New York in 1900. As evidence against his "Irishness" stands the deletion of many Irish essays from those available for him to anthologize and the fact that most of the Irish essays which were anthologized appear in the first two books. Nevertheless many Irish-Americans today still claim Finley Peter Dunne as one of their chief spokesmen. Georg Mann writes that "in his own person, Dunne was as much of an Irish patriot as Mr. Dooley himself" and cites the passage in the *Memoirs* in which Dunne reports that a lethargic audience was aroused at the mention of Castlereagh and adds, "It is well that these ancient passions be kept alive."[15] Lawrence McCaffrey in *The Irish Diaspora* (1976) commends Dunne as "one of the first Irishmen to bridge the gap between journalism and literature."[16] Charles Fanning concludes, "When Dunne moved on to a New York-based commentary on the wider world, Irish-American Nationalism in Chicago lost a valuable critic."[17] Thomas N. Brown in *Irish-American Nationalism* (1966) recalls the negative effects of the Comic Irishman and the Professional Irishman which made the Irish voice of the 1920s "too easily discounted as mere Hibernianism." But "Finley Peter Dunne was able to break through the hostility and bring his ironies to a national audience but only by adopting the device of speaking through a Comic Irishman—'Mr. Dooley' of Archey Road, Chicago. The device had obvious limitations and, in any case,

Dunne himself was soon absorbed into the Establishment."[18]

From a position in the Establishment, Dunne in his later years occasionally returned to Irish themes, with the effect of keeping Mr. Dooley very much in character; the last of his anthologies, *Mr. Dooley on Making a Will and Other Necessary Evils* (1919), contains two Irish essays. In "On the Orange Revolution of 1914," Mr. Dooley recalls his "Uncle Mike" of the Belfast shipyards, repeats that "a charge iv joynt powdher" improves the approachability of the English, and begins with satirizing the means by which the British prime minister seeks the Irish vote. To John Redmond (1856–1918) the minister promises "a larger navy, restoration iv th' statue iv Oliver Cromwell, repairs on Canterbury Cathedral, army increase and fin'lly free passes f'r all Irish members to th' British Museem." When John Redmond threatens to withhold Irish support, the prime minister remembers Home Rule, for perhaps the year 1968.

In truth John Redmond, originally a Parnellite, in 1914 accepted a policy of a divided Ireland, which became reality in 1921. Before 1914, Irish attempts at coercion, always marred by misplaced zealotry, reached a low point when in June 1914 members of the Catholic organization, the Ancient Order of Hibernians, attacked a party of picnicking Protestant Sunday-school children. Reprisals were carried out in the largely Protestant Belfast shipyards. For this and other complicated reasons, Dooley moves in his commentary from the Irish acceptance of a "measure of Home Rule" instead of independence to a discussion of the mixture of religion and politics. "Rillijon is a quare thing," Mr. Dooley says. "Be itsilf it's all right. But sprinkle a little pollyticks into it an' dinnymite is bran flour compared with it." As for the concerns of the little man, Mr. Dooley explains, "ye'd wondher why a hero that's calkin' seams or forgin' bolts in a Belfast ship yard wud care who ruled Ireland. But he's got an idea in his head that if th' fellows that lead us took a holt they'd do th' same to him that his leaders did to us whin they were on top"—a statement which accurately summarizes dedication to a force which opposes one's own basic principles.

The Irish volunteers organized to defend Ulster *against* Home Rule by the close of 1913 numbered 100,000 in the force, paradoxical as this seems. In fact the "Revolution" was an Orange establishment of provisional government in Belfast to prevent the implementation of a Home Rule bill that, although much altered, originally intended improvement by way of self-government for the Irish. Edward Norman recalls that Winston Churchill described the provisional government as "a self-elected body, composed of persons who, to put it plainly, are engaged in a treasonable conspiracy."[19] Likewise Mr. Dooley calls the Orange Revolution "th' gr-reatest joke that has iver happened in th' wurruld."

His last essay "On St. Patrick's Day" pictures Mr. Dooley now too aged and fatigued to participate but standing on the curb with two of Hennessy's children on his shoulders and another on his head. As he puts it, "I've got to a time iv life whin me feet ar-re almost stationary. They stopped walkin' long ago. I have to tow thim now." The tune Garryowen, with allusion to General Custer and others, he pronounces one that has "made war a pleasure in ivry part iv the wurruld." Of the other viewers and participants, Mr. Dooley reports, "Schwartzmeister comes up wearin' a green cravat an' a yard long green badge an' says: 'Faugh-a-ballagh, Herr Dooley,' which he thinks is Irish f'r 'Good Mornin'.' Me good frind Ikey Cohen jines me an' I obsarve he's left th' glassware at home an' is wearin' emeralds in th' front iv his shirt. Like as not along will come little Hip Lung fr'm down th' sthreet with a package iv shirts undhr his ar-rm, an' a green ribbon in his cue."[20] All nationalities become Irish on this day.

Dunne, while writing on international events, retained Dooley's Irishness as a vantage point, and even in the last essays in 1926 Dooley precedes an observation with "Gael that I am. . . ."

CHAPTER 3

"Simple Like th' Air
or th' Deep Sea"

W HAT various historians debate, deny, and disagree on seems
perfectly clear to the analysts of American humor. Walter
Blair in *Native American Humor* (1937; rev. 1960) pronounces
Mr. Dooley "a crackerbox philosopher with an Irish accent";[1] in
Horse Sense in American Humor (1942) he writes, "An Irishman
from the top of his white head to the tips of his toes, he had all
the prejudices, whether justifiable or not, of his race."[2]
Succeeding authors tend to quote or to paraphrase Walter Blair
and thus to perpetuate his estimate of Dunne and of Dooley,
including his errors. Two problems emerge in the works which
attempt to place Dunne in the history of American humor: the
analysts frequently confine themselves to Dunne's Chicago days,
the days before 1900 and before he achieved national fame; and
they tend to rely for a selection of his essays on Elmer Ellis's *Mr.
Dooley at His Best* (1938). The first problem can be observed in
Blair's comment on William Jennings Bryan to the effect that on
him "Dooley at times affectionately bestowed the Irish name
O'Brien" (*Horse Sense,* 252); actually Dooley was writing about
the Chicago alderman William J. O'Brien, and later, in *Mr.
Dooley on Making a Will and Other Necessary Evils,* Dunne
satirized William Jennings Bryan under the heading "On the
Power of Music." That oratory could sway even Mr. Dooley was
both an admission and a lament: "I voted f'r him whin votin' f'r
him was wan way iv proclaimin' to th' wurruld that I cudden't
pay me room rint. I voted f'r him whin 'twas th' same as tellin' th'
groceryman that he gave me credit at his peril. There is plenty iv
room f'r all th' thoughts in th' wurruld under that splendid dome.
If he doesn't care to exercise thim it's his own business" (*Will,*
71–81). Lesser space devoted to Bryan in other essays reiterated

51

Dooley's central point, as in "On 'The Gift of Oratory' ": "Th'
night I heerd Willum Jennings Bryan's cross-iv-goold speech I
wint over to Hogan's house an' picked out th' chune with wan
finger on th' pianny" (*Will*, 131–43). Dunne himself recognized
the second problem when he commented that *Mr. Dooley at His
Best* gave too much space to the Spanish-American War[3]—
though the war did change the course of Dunne's life and of
American hisstory.

I   *American Humor*

What constitutes American humor, what makes it distinctively
American, develops from the uniqueness of the American nation,
a uniqueness which in the nineteenth century flourished in
regionalism and in dialect writing; dialect, at least, served to
distinguish "Amurriken" from English English. The new nation
also demanded of its people what Walter Blair calls "horse
sense" (gumption or mother-wit), and he found for it an early
exponent in Benjamin Franklin, whose Poor Richard (1732–57)
in broad outlines introduces Dunne's Mr. Dooley:

Poor Richard . . . was a man of little book learning but much rich
experience. His experience made possible his wise remarks about life —
whether those remarks were in line with general moral standards or not
and whether they dealt with money-making or sex, long visits or the
buncombe about temperance. He figured out what would work, he told
his readers—and that was morality for them. Poor Richard became
known and respected by the thousands of buyers of his almanac
because he could give them news, in a witty way, of his useful
discoveries. (*Horse Sense*, 14).

Many a humorist, remarks Blair, later used such a lay preacher—
men like Josh Billings or Mr. Dooley or Will Rogers, to cite only
three.

The necessity to deal with practical matters in a new and
developing nation nurtured horse sense or common sense and the
cult of the ignorant, often evident in a profound distrust of book
learning. As a result, Norris W. Yates, in attempting to clarify the
trends and types of twentieth-century American humor, dis-
tinguishes three, of whom two can be unlettered: the rustic sage,
a crackerbarrel type; the respectable citizen who owns his own
business and thinks rationally; and the worried Little Man. Of

these, he writes, "the best known specialists in 'low' language were self-educated midwesterners. During the first fifteen years or so of the new century, the urbane wit and humor of . . . cultivated easterners was overshadowed by the satire in dialect or slang of George Ade, Finley Peter Dunne, and Kin Hubbard, writers whose language identifies them with the crackerbox tradition but whose basic character type in every case had many traits of the solid citizen as well as of the crackerbarrel philosopher (this citizen, however, was denied by his authors the culture to be had from books)."[4] As if to confirm Yates's impression of midwesterners leading the century's humorists, Bernard Duffy, writing for *The Comic Imagination in American Literature* (1973), places Dunne under the heading "Humor, Chicago Style" and among Eugene Field, George Ade, Ring Lardner, and Keith Preston.[5]

When the new nation was still opening the West and settling the Midwest, it registered simultaneously the impact of central government, converting territories into states, and the rise of industry, converting countryside into suburban lots. Coexistent with these local changes came others from the world and the environment itself: the feminist movement, "progressive" education, Darwinian evolution. Yates summarizes the impact of these developments in his phrase, "the shrinkage of the 'common American.'" All these are topics which Dunne and other humorists eventually must deal with.

Close to Dunne was George Ade, writing in the vernacular, combining as did Dunne the crackerbox philosopher with the substantial citizen, though Dunne scarcely found, as did George Ade, the vernacular to be like "gorging on forbidden fruit."[6] Occasionally Ade's and Dunne's topics overlapped, as in essays on the new woman and on the Anglo-Saxon. Perhaps the chief distinction from Dunne's Mr. Dooley was Ade's development of the successful American, a "composite" man, as Yates phrases it, who comes from a small town and achieves a position of eminence and wealth in business. Yates concludes his analysis of Ade's man, "He himself would not have been trapped in the assembly line or the office cages because, although ordinarily a quiet fellow, he could put up a brash front in pursuit of the main chance."[7] Mr. Dooley, by contrast, quietly operates his pub and dispenses his philosophy, often with only Hennessy, a steel mill common laborer, as listener. George Ade's composite man grew in family as well as in business; Mr. Dooley remained a bachelor with consistently moderate income and no intention of rising in the world.

George Ade, who began his "Fables in Slang" just as Dooley was becoming famous, called Dunne's work "caustic and witty." Franklin P. Adams, writing a "Foreword" for *Mr. Dooley at His Best*, quotes Ade on Dunne and adds, "Few popular writers ever wrote more maliciously and bitterly than Lardner and Dunne."[8] On the other hand, Blair and Hill found, among the members of the Whitechapel Club, underlying "cynicism and disillusionment" in their humorous productions *except* for Dunne's Mr. Dooley and George Ade's *Fables*.[9] Ade, who collected his fables in ten volumes, found his target in "the pretensions of pomposities of intellectual frauds"; Dunne's scope was broader, for Dunne satirized any common man, himself included, along with the entirety of nations as well as their leaders. No system, bureaucracy, or country was too remote for his apt reduction of it to Dooley terms. In *Mr. Dooley's Philosophy*, for example, appears the "Servant Girl Problem," which Dunne knew from personal experience but which Dooley expounds through visitors in his pub and through published discussions. The visitor, who protests he cannot keep servants while paying them little, was himself, as Hennessy reveals, a gentleman's man in the old country. Dooley explains, "Th' more ye ought to be a servant ye'ersilf th' more difficult 'tis f'r ye to get along with servants." In the same volume, Dooley returns to a theme formerly expounded in relation to the Philippines, a theme of American's egotistic compulsion to bend other peoples to its own ways. He concludes, regarding "The Chinese Situation," "Annyhow, 'tis a good thing f'r us they ain't Christyans an' haven't larned properly to sight a gun,"[10] an attitude he continued in "The Future of China" (*Philosophy*, 91-95).

Among those humorists whose names frequently appear with Dunne's, George Ade became a successful playwright, Ring Lardner a writer of short stories; and Eugene Field wrote dialect poems and children's poems (including the famous "Little Boy Blue" and "The Gingham Dog and the Calico Cat") as well as his column "Sharps and Flats" and entered an area Dunne is not known to have entered: Field wrote bawdy poems for his friends. Perhaps because Dunne entered no literary field other than journalism, he more than other humorists became associated with his literary creation. Such statements as Walter Blair's calling Mr. Dooley a writer reveal the frequent confusion of creator and created: "Mr. Dooley . . . was a humorous ally of a group of crusaders who shared many of his liberal views and made good money by putting them into print" (*Horse Sense*, 252).

II   *Books Atop the Crackerbox*

A question even more controversial than the contradictory discussions of cynicism emerges—the question of Dooley's ignorance. If *seeming* ignorance be accepted as a basic technique of much humor, the question may be easily dismissed; but in these analyses the implications of the charge extend even to Dooley's character and morality. Blair writes with some inaccuracy,

> Entirely unread in anything but the newspapers, knowing nothing of the world of books, he was likely to call an acolyte "an alkali," an encyclopedia "a bicyclopedia," and when he quoted what he thought was the German national anthem, it came out "Ich vice nit wauss allus bay doitan." His ignorance of books led him to ascribe all sorts of fine sayings to his friend Hogan, giving him credit for all the phrases he had quoted. . . . His ethical standards, worked out during a rough life in his ward, were those of the wrong side of the tracks—he might use loaded dice or pass bad money at times to cheat a neighbor he disliked; he had a liking for a good hard brick to settle an argument; he accepted vote-buying and crookedness as normal parts of politics. (*Horse Sense*, 247–48)

To the limitations of Dooley's environment Blair also ascribes the friendly terms by which Dooley discusses the president or a queen, though such discussion is legitimate in the terms of the Dooley role as reader of newspapers and as bartender.

In the same vein of criticism Norris Yates writes that "Not only does Mr. Dooley's reason desert him at times—as when he wants to throw bricks at various old enemies—but he can't possibly keep well informed. All he reads is the 'pa'apers,' and the data in his mind are a weird mixture of truth and misinformation." Further, Yates speaks of Dunne's implication that Dooley's intelligence "must be accompanied by humility as well as by information." Yates writes that Dooley is "foolish in pretending that he and Morgan are on familiar terms" and that

"Dooley could make shrewd comment in the role of the levelheaded citizen even though at times he betrays the ignorance and confusion that, Dunne felt, too often impeded this levelheadedness as a social force" (*American Humorist*, 87–93). (Yates's source for Dunne's feeling is not given.)

All these statements can be read with exactly the opposite view. Newspaper content includes book reviews and often articles which quote from books; verbal approximations and bilingual puns have long been intentional sources of humor, and Dooley is witty enough to mispronounce a word with intention and to forge a pun. Hogan frequently exhibits the talents of a real Shakespeare-quoting customer Dunne knew in the original James McGarry's pub. In the face of individual and societal corruption, Dooley apparently assumes that fine words will be ineffectual weapons (otherwise social and criminal codes long in existence would have nullified all possibilities of corruption), and he does advocate force when he knows that all other measures will fail. The throwing of bricks constitutes sound literary techniques of hyperbole and metaphor; without emotion, Dooley would be less than human. If reason did not occasionally fail him, he would be nothing more than mechanical.

It is true that two of Dunne's essays on books promote Dooley's opposition to particular kinds of literature; the comments betray, also, Dunne's childhood with quality literature, especially Thackeray and Macaulay, though Mr. Dooley does not mention these writers. Dooley maintains that "They're on'y three books in th' wurruld worth readin',—Shakespeare, th' Bible, an' Mike Ahearn's histhry iv Chicago," and takes Father Kelly to task for peddling misleading novels, of which he says books will make the children near-sighted and round-shouldered. "Ye're going to have thim believe that, if they behave thimsilves an' lead a virchous life, they'll marry rich an' go to Congress. They'll wake up some day, an' find out that gettin' money an behavin' ye'ersilf don't always go together." His conclusion, Father Kelly's rebuttal, places literature in the position of a golden mean: "'Tis betther to be comfortable at home thin to go to th' circus, an' 'tis betther to go to th' circus thin to r-read anny book. But 'tis betther to r-read a book thin to want to go to th' circus an' not be able to,' he says." That literature has power to alter the mind Mr. Dooley acknowledges: "Th' Apostles' Creed niver was as con-vincin' to me afther I larned to r-read it as it was whin I cudden't read it, but believed it" (*Peace*, 105-10). "A Little Essay on Books" continues the thesis that books of poor quality cripple the body and sedate the mind. Hogan, Dooley says, is "wan iv th' best-read an' mos' ignorant men I know." On the other hand Dooley's (and no doubt Dunne's) father "was th' mos' accyrate man in th' wurruld with litthers. He found th' range nachrally, and he cud wing anny wan iv us with th' 'Lives iv th' Saints' as far as he cud see" (*Observations*, 3-11).

Dooley paid honor to the world of books and newspapers in his essay "Adventure," about a life of fantasy; although he does not mention the printed word in this essay, the topics he covers, imagining himself as hero, can be a part of his own existence only through acquaintance with the written word. All his adventure occurs while he sits at home, comfortable in his living room: "Ye can make ye'ersilf as brave as ye want an' as cool, ye avide mussin' ye'er clothes, ye flavor with danger to suit th' taste, an' ye get a good dale more applause an' get it quicker thin th' other kind iv hayro. F'r manny years I've shot all me tigers fr'm this rockin' chair" (*Observations*, 247-49).

To belie Dooley's ignorance of books, one need only consult the introduction to one of Dunne's most famous essays, that one entitled "A Book Review," which discusses Theodore Roosevelt's *Rough Riders* (1899). Mr. Dooley says, "Whin a rale good book comes along I'm as quick as anny wan to say it isn't so bad, an' this here book is fine." A very amusing account of Roosevelt's conceit about winning the Spanish-American War single-handedly, the essay offers excellent literary criticism and a famous conclusion which delighted Roosevelt's friends and family: "No man that bears a gredge agin himsilf 'll iver be governor iv a state. An' if Teddy done it all he ought to say so an' relieve th' suspinse. But if I was him I'd call th' book 'Alone in Cubia' " (*Philosophy*, 13-18).

The Harvard Classics, popularly known as "Dr. Eliot's Five-Foot Shelf" in honor of Harvard's president (1869-1909) Charles W. Eliot, should have been made to order for Mr. Dooley, since the fifty volumes were designed to provide college education for those without. Mr. Dooley flattered President Eliot in this fashion: "He real-izes that th' first thing to have in a libry is a shelf. Fr'm time to time this can be decorated with lithrachure. But th' shelf is th' main thing. Otherwise th' libry may get mixed up with readin' matther on th' table. Th' shelf shud thin be nailed

to th' wall iliven feet fr'm th' flure an' hermetically sealed."
Commenting on "Milton's Arryopatigica" as "a Greek gur-rul
who becomes th' iditor iv a daily newspaper," he goes on to say,
"I mane I niver go f'r a long journey without a copy iv Milton's
Agropapitica in me pocket. I have lent it to brakemen an' they
have invaryably returned it. . . . I'll bet ye eight dollars that if
ye wait till th' stores let out ye can go on th' sthreet an' out iv ivry
ten men ye meet at laste two, an' I'll take odds on three, have
niver aven heerd iv this pow'ful thragedy." On Milton's fame,
that he was "a pote as well as an author an' blind at that, an',
what is more, held a prom'nent pollytickal job," Dooley asks with
many others who would no doubt exclaim, "My sentiments
exactly!" "I wondher if two hundred years fr'm now people will
cease to talk iv Willum Jennings Bryan. He won't, but will they?"
(*Mr. Dooley Says*, 135-43). The same essay contains astute
criticism of heroes and villains as standard literary fare. Mr.
Dooley asks, "Who wud make a confirmed reader th' cashier iv a
bank? Ye'd divide ye'er customers into villyans an' heroes an' ye
wudden't lend money to th' villyans. An' thin ye'd be wrong aven
if ye were right. F'r th' villyans wud be more apt to have th'
money to bring back thin th' heroes,' says I."

In the same volume, "The Call of the Wild" satirizes nature
writers William J. Long (b. 1866), who wrote *Briar Patch
Philosophy* (1906) and other volumes, and John Burroughs
(1837-1921), whose nature essays began to appear in the
Atlantic in 1865 and who published numerous books on birds and
boughs and fields. The lack of plausibility especially offends Mr.
Dooley's senses: "Has this man iver been outside iv an aviary? I
doubt it. Here he has a guinea pig killin' a moose be bitin' it in th'
ear. Now it is notoryous to anny lover iv th' wilds, anny man with
a fondness f'r these monarchs iv forests, that no moose can be kilt
be a wound in th' ear. I have shot a thousand in th' ear with no
bad effects beyond makin' thim hard iv hearin'." A peculiar
talent is the relationship of almost any topic to newsworthy
contemporaries: "No wolf cud kill a bear th' way Willum J. Long
iv Stamford has described. A bear has th' sthrongest throat iv
anny crather in th' wurruld, barrin' Bryan. Why, I wud hate to
have to sthrangle a bear. I did wanst, but I had writer's cramp f'r
months aftherward." The satire includes Theodore Roosevelt's
books on hunting wildlife in Africa: "An' Tiddy Rosenfelt stood
alone in th' primeval forest. Suddenly there was a sound in th'

bushes. He loaded his pen, an' thin give a gasp iv relief, f'r down th' glade come his thrusted ally, John Burroughs, leadin' captive th' pair iv wild white mice that had so long preyed on th' counthry" (*Mr. Dooley Says*, 180-92). By the time Dunne wrote an excellent review—consistently funny and accurate—of the *Intimate Papers of Colonel House* (1926), satirizing President Wilson's self-appointed political liaison officer, he made no apologies for enjoying a good book, but recommended that this one be kept for throwing at burglars (*Liberty*, May 8, 1926, 33-36).

Perhaps the best single and brief introduction to the character of Mr. Dooley is that written as "Introduction" by Dunne himself, dated January 1, 1936, for *Mr. Dooley at His Best*, when he could look back on the entire career of his creation. Here he tells about the brilliant assemblage of talent patronizing McGarry's public house, among whom "one of the gayest of our crowd was a reporter who could quote Shakespere [sic] for any event or occasion. Leaning easily against the bar he would parry every argument with an apposite line from the poet" (*At His Best*, xxi). Certainly Mr. Dooley, based in the reality of James McGarry, was not ignorant.

To defend Dooley's rendition of the German national anthem, and to consider it as humor rather than ignorance, the best approach may be to turn to one of Dunne's editorials for the *Chicago Journal* (April 21, 1898), a "serious" tribute to the fiftieth anniversary of Chicago's leading German newspaper:

Best Wishes to the Staats Zeitung
It gives reason of congratulating Staats Zeitung by its jubilitiveness after this fifty yearen of loftyrightstruggle. The heart to us shimmers after incandescencehelt like a notimitation Halbach coalvaporlamp with the grosse noblefeelung from our kostbar neighbor. We to her through this one hoping of in comingtime cordialityheit, extend our magnanimity and burn with admirable wishes after her evergreathood and prosperity. May she great be and much money make.[11]

Bilingual puns in German and English, familiar to many through the Katzenjammer Kids of the comic strips, reached a high point in the work of another Chicago journalist, Kurt M. Stein, who around 1911 popularized Limburger Lyrics and Gemixt Pickles. Beginning his *Die Schönste Lengevitch* (1923), he tells about conversations among German-Americans "in which the speakers firmly believed they were talking their original native tongue, when, as a matter of fact, they were far out outschoning my wildest flights." He tried, therefore, "a new and international language which would use enough familiar words to give a faint clue to what it was all about, and yet retain enough strange ones so it could be sent through the mails."[12]

Dooley's version of a German national tune (the national anthem, as Blair interpreted it) appears among other places in an early essay, "On a Quarrel between England and Germany," which is filled with bilingual puns and humorous imitations in German, English, and Gaelic. Schwartzmeister and Dooley as competitors had been enemies, as Dunne admits, "based upon racial differences," but greeted each other politely in public: "Good-nobben [Gut Morgan], Hair Schwartzmeister, an' vas magst too yet, my brave bucko!" To this Mr. Schwartzmeister invariably replied, "Py chapers, Tooley, where you haf been all der time, py chapers?" But on this occasion Chicago politics, with its various ethnic groups, brings the two together and makes them warm friends: " 'Schwartz, me lieber frind,' I says, 'here's a health to th' imp'ror, hock,' says I. 'Slanthu' [Gaelic *sláinte*, Health!], says he; an' we had wan." They fairly brim over with good intentions: " 'Faugh a ballagh' [Gaelic *Fág an beallach*, Leave the road!], says he, meanin' to be polite. 'Lieb vaterland [Dear Fatherland], says I." They seal their friendship with teaching each other national airs, in the case of Mr. Dooley, the "Shan-van-Voght," and in the case of Mr. Schwartzmeister, "Ich vice nit wauss allus bay doitan'." Dooley thus gives his version of a popular German song, the "Die Lorelei" of Heinrich Heine, under the title by which it was best known when put to music by Friedrich Silcher, *"Ich weiss nicht was soll es bedeuten"* (*Peace*, 213–17).

Close enough to Dunne and Dooley to create confusion in the minds of some readers today are the "Plunkitt of Tammany Hall" essays by William L. Riordon, another Irish-American journalist (for the *New York Evening Post*) writing about another Irish-American politician; Riordon collected the newspaper essays in a book published in 1905. Though not written in dialect, Plunkitt's talks as recorded by Riordon did contain his dropped *g*'s in his *ing* endings and his ungrammatical structures. The Democratic politician George Washington Plunkitt (1842–1924), born of immigrant parents, grew up in an Irish neighborhood in New York; he quit school at the age of eleven "after 'three winters of it' " and later owned a butcher shop and became a contractor. As William Riordon noted in the preface to the collected talks, Plunkitt in 1870 held the places of "Assemblyman, Alderman, Police Magistrate and County Supervisor and drew three salaries at once." Commenting most frequently on New York politics and national topics, as Dunne did on Chicago politics and national topics, he maintained office and public rostrum together at a bootblack stand in the County Courthouse, just as Dooley held forth behind the bar in his tavern. Instead of assuming a role in delivering satire, however, as Dooley did frequently, Plunkitt believed what he said and lived as selfishly, taking advantage of the public, as Dooley observed other politicians to do. The first essay in the collection quotes Plunkitt as saying, "There's an honest graft, and I'm an example of how it works. I might sum up the whole thing by sayin': 'I seen my opportunities and I took 'em.' " His idea of the American way is to beat the other person: "Ain't it perfectly honest to charge a good price and make a profit on my investment and foresight? Of course, it is. Well, that's honest graft."

Other topics came close to some of Dunne's: one, for example, entitled "The Successful Politician Does Not Drink" and another, entitled "Concerning Excise," opposed the Raines liquor law for oppressing the New York state liquor dealers. Moreover, just as Dunne and Dooley have been frequently confused, Arthur Mann, writing an introduction for the 1962 edition of the Plunkitt essays, comments, "It is hard to say who deserves to be called the author of the book. The substance is Plunkitt's, but the conception, the organization, the artistry, and the actual writing are Riordon's." So successfully did journalist William R. Riordon present his subject that Plunkitt became known as a political sage; and, just as Dunne's essays have been used in college courses, the book when reissued in 1948 became required reading "in the more sophisticated college courses in American government."[13] After Dunne moved to New York, he too frequently referred to the Tammany political machine; the essay "Some Political Observations" treats that topic (*Opinions*, 171–77).

In all at least three of Dunne's essays may be favorably compared with those of William Riordan on Plunkitt, and other

essays offer speculation about comparison. Dunne's account of
Flanagan's winning an election (*Peace*, 111-17) describes the
techniques of personal attention to constituents that Plunkitt
reports as used by Patrick Divver (Dooley's "Divry") and by
Thomas F. Foley (*Plunkitt*, 95-96); these are exactly the
techniques which Plunkitt seriously recommends for winning
votes and which, according to his diary, he himself employed
(*Plunkitt*, 91-93). In "A Brand from the Burning," Dooley could
well be describing Plunkitt, who said, "Real estate is one of my
specialties" (*Plunkitt*, 62); Dooley said real estate "includes near
ivrything fr'm vagrancy to manslaughter" (*Hearts*, 66-71).
Dunne's essay "Some Political Observations" has Tammany as its
announced topic, however.

Plunkitt repeatedly used the term "hayseed" to refer to any
politician from Albany or elsewhere outside the Tammany
machine; Dooley says, "A Chicago pollytician in Noo York wud
be like a short change man from a dime museem box-office at a
meetin' iv th' Standard ile comp'ny." Plunkitt spoke against drink
in politics and insisted that both "Big Tim" and "Little Tim"
Sullivan never took a drink but owned liquor stores (*Plunkitt*,
79). Dooley says, "if I had a little liquor store down in Noo York,
I'd be in pollytics up to me chin," and later in the essay he names
"Tim Soolyvan." Plunkitt bragged about his fraternizing with
Republicans and getting jobs from them and said, "Me and the
Republicans are enemies just one day in the year—election day.
Then we fight tooth and nail. The rest of the time it's live and let
live with us" (*Plunkitt*, 38). Dooley said that, contrary to Chicago
party loyalties, "Down there a man has a r-right to change his
mind if he has a mind to change it, d'ye mind, Hinnissy." Plunkitt
refers often to Richard "Boss" Croker, who managed New York
politics from 1886 to 1902, whom Dooley characterized as a true
politician:

He's lile to his frinds, but he has no frinds. He's consistent but he ain't
obstinate. He's out f'r th' money an' he don't care who knows it if
they've had a part iv it thimsilves. He's larned that they'se a fam'ly
enthrance to th' bank as well as to th' saloon. He started in life thinkin'
all men was as bad as himsilf but experryence has con-vinced him they
ar-re worse. He's larned that men can talk thimsilves to death an' he's
willin' to let thim do it. He's heerd iv th' bonds iv love an' frindship an
feelty but he prefers a cash forfeit. He's me ideel statesman, so far.

His house in England adjoins the Duke of Cornwall "an' him an' th' king can be seen anny hour iv th' afternoon on th' verandah iv th' Tower iv London talkin' it over." Plunkitt's Victor Dowling must be Dooley's "Doctor Doocetray, pro-fissor iv Greek an' Latin in th' Univarsity," whose dedication to politics among the Greeks and Latins in his district enables him to "hand it to thim in their own language" (see *Plunkitt,* 48, 52). In the essay Dooley names "Divry, Carroll, 'Tim' Soolyvan, Moxy Freeman" and "Tityrus T. Wooley." On the prevalence of vice in New York City, Dooley says, "They'se no more crooked people there thin annywhere else but they'se enough that wud be ashamed to confiss that they weren't crooked, to give a majority" (*Opinions,* 171-77).

Plunkitt's discussion of "honest graft" and his taking opportunity comes close to Dooley's definition of Andrew Carnegie's view of opportunity (see "Mr. Carnegie's Gift" in *Opinions,* 145-50). Dooley's essay "On Wall Street," about the Titans of Finance, features a bootblack at the Alhambra Hotel, one who "had made a small fortune in stocks" as if in association with Plunkitt at the New York County Court House off Foley Square (see *Opinions,* 189-95).

Like Dunne also, Plunkitt distrusted reform. Speaking of Lincoln Steffens' book *The Shame of the Cities* (1904), he said, "Steffens means well, but, like all reformers, he don't know how to make distinctions" (*Plunkitt,* 29).

A mixture of languages could be expected in any writing on immigrant America, around the turn of the century. In addition to the Irish-dialect content of Dunne's essays, however, Dunne's bilingual puns advanced from German and Gaelic for Schwartzmeister and Dooley, to French in the Dreyfus essays, and to Italian for the Mussolini essay of 1926, but throughout Dunne's career Latin for the legal content. For example, "peak capias" combines the yachtsman's peaked cap with *peak* as part of the hull at bow or stern and *capias* as a legal writ. The French *soupçon* becomes "soupcan" in "The Food We Eat"; the Greek chorus at Yale "chased th' fleet fut ball an' th' more fleet aorist" (*Opinions,* 199-204). Certainly his skill in language sets Dunne apart from many other American humorists, even those who wrote on topics similar to his, and even though others did create neologisms.

The homespun quality of Dunne's essays appears to great

advantage in "Famous Men," in which Dooley responds to Andrew Carnegie's search by listing the qualities which have significance for various persons in Archey Road. According to the elusive nature of fame, he eliminates goodness, bravery, fortune, and foresight as qualities contributing to it; with the last he cites Columbus, who bumped into the United States, "th' poor deluded Eyetalyan thinkin' Chiny was somewheres near Phillydelphy." Speculating about the possibility that Hennessy might become famous, he says, "Posterity, Hinissy, somethimes likes to vote f'r th' dark horse." Posterity would recognize that in Hennessy "Now f'r th' first time there appeared a man who cud listen." But Hennessy plays his part with great humor: "But I haven't been listenin'," says Mr. Hennessy (*Will*, 17-26).

When turning seriously to the topic of heroes, Dooley finds that "Histhry, as Hogan wud say, has a long mim'ry but 'tis inaccrate." Dooley tells the story of the death of Julius Caesar, but the story has now been revised by a professor of history. "Th' further ye get away fr'm anny peeryod th' betther ye can write about it," he says. "Ye are not subjict to interruptions be people that were there." He revises the history of Nero, for "Th' thruth is, that he practised wan if th' first principles iv relligon, which is that th' good are betther dead" (*Will*, 102-13).

Far from being ignorant, the essays make the great truths and the current events applicable to each person. Further, looking at the essays now, one cannot imagine that readers laughed at Dooley but rather that they laughed at the images he created and at his satire of persons they knew by reputation if not by intimate acquaintance. Recognition—of persons, of neologisms, of puns—must occur before laughter; and certainly the success of Mr. Dooley was not achieved because of ignorance, rather because of knowledge, and especially his own. His readers of necessity must have found (and still find) truth, not ignorance, in his speech. This truth must be factual and not merely philosophical. Analysis of a single essay, moreover, will invariably show a staggering quantity of information packed into a single piece (see, for example, the analysis of "On the Destruction of Cervera's Fleet" in the next chapter). With the Dunne format, Dooley renders all this substantial fact and wisdom with decided unpretentiousness (perhaps what Yates meant by "humility"). Indeed, oratory calculated to sway deeply the emotions and superficially the minds of the multitude, as in the example of

William Jennings Bryan, earns nothing but repeated verbal abuse from Mr. Dooley; it is part of the sham he opposes. Further, the quantity of information Dooley possesses he would disdain to use for advancement partly because that part of his life is over and largely because undesirable politicians have surrounded him with examples of its misuse and abuse. Because the great and the powerful have clarified neither their own aims nor improved by the strength of their social and intellectual positions the tottering gait of "progress," what Yates calls Mr. Dooley's misinformation, ignorance, and confusion are all useful artistic touches and necessary accoutrements of abstract truth, especially the truth of the human condition.

III   *The Dunne-Dooley World*

Two problems seem to contribute to confusing assessments of the character of Mr. Dooley: one, the difficulty of acceptance of verisimilitude, and the other the separation between Dunne's personal life and that of his creation.

Perhaps the quality of verisimilitude can be recognized only by readers who have personally known a living example of Irish wit and humor, a person who takes intimately, even though he occupies a humble position, the sallies of the wealthy and powerful, a person on whom their public pronouncements have direct bearing. To such a one, every public figure, even though remote or undesirable, is a "frind," an acquaintance, a part of all he has met, a part of his universe. At the same time that the humorist participates vicariously in the affairs of the great, he renders judgments against their pomposity and their too-human failings; but above all he reduces them to his own terms, and thereby makes himself an interpreter, explaining how the individual can relate to the international and the remote. The man of true wit, moreover, is never to be humiliated in a personal confrontation. The reductionism seems particularly Irish when compared with this story by Stephen Birmingham as told in *Real Lace* (1973) about the wealthy American McDonnells, one of whom married Henry Ford:

there is a story told in the local pub . . . of a rich McDonnell who came back, a long time ago, to visit relatives and old friends in Ireland. At the pub, this McDonnell encountered an old schoolmate from boyhood days, recognized him, clapped the fellow on the back, and said, "Paddy, I remember in the third grade when you came to school in your first pair of shoes!" Slyly the Drumlisher eyed the American for a moment and said, "Yes, and I remember you asking me what they were."[14]

While Dunne's Mr. Dooley remained the stay-at-home Drumlisher, Dunne's own life brought him into association, in spite of Yates's objections to Morgan, with people of Morgan's stature; Dunne was, in effect, the rich McDonnell. How Dunne ingeniously integrated the level of his own society with that of Mr. Dooley becomes an interesting study, especially in the books published after 1900.

Dunne begins the essay "Glory" with Mr. Dooley's comment to Hennessy: "Hogan has been in here this afternoon, an' I've heerd more scandal talked thin I iver thought was in the wurrld." Over Hennessy's protests that he might be the subject of such gossip, Dooley reassures him: "Ye needn't worry. We didn't condiscend to talk about annywan iv ye'er infeeryor station. If ye want to be th' subjick iv our scand'lous discoorse ye'd betther go out an' make a repytation. No, sir, our talk was entirely about th' gr-reat an' illusthrees an' it ran all th' way f'rm Julius Cayzar to Ulysses Grant." His analysis of human psychology explains the great and the humble in their necessary union and by implication the mythology of the Procrustean bed: "We'd all perish iv humilyation if th' gr-reat men iv th' wurruld didn't have nachral lowdown thraits. If they don't happen to possess thim, we make some up f'r thim. We allow no man to tower over us. Wan way or another we level th' wurruld to our own height. If we can't reach th' hero's head we cut off his legs" (*Mr. Dooley Says,* 14–24). (In like vein, seventy years later, below-stairs employees of the White House make their fortunes writing on the personal affairs of presidents' wives.)

Yet another factor uniting the high life and the low life is a profound belief in American democracy and the principle of the worth of the common man. People of many occupations frequent Mr. Dooley's pub, and others of varied ethnic origins exist within his range of vision. People were not then so much concerned as now with the slights of ethnic and racial slurs, as evidenced by Roosevelt's candid comments on the "negro" regiment in the Spanish-American War (see his *Rough Riders*). But Roosevelt in a six-page letter to Dunne (November 23, 1904) called Dunne a "laughing philosopher" and reacted to Dunne's labeling the election an " 'Anglo-Saxon' Triumph"; at the same time Roosevelt defended and reiterated his own ethnic indifference: "I do not give a darn whether [the] name happens to be Casey, or Schwartzmeister, or Van Rennsselaer, or Peabody. . . . I protest . . . discrimination against or sneering at men because they happen to be descended from people who came over here some three centuries ago, whether they landed at Plymouth, or at the mouth of the Hudson,"[15] and so on for six pages. The latter alludes to Roosevelt's Dutch origins, which for some readers Dunne had given a Jewish cast. Dunne writes in his memoirs,

When I commenced to write Dooley articles about Theodore Roosevelt I made Mr. Dooley call him "Rosenfelt," which I thought was about the way a Mr. Dooley would pronounce the name. *The London Spectator*, which had been most generous in appreciation of these pieces, severely took me to task for "alluding to the President's Jewish ancestry." I showed the article to the President and he laughed. . . . "No," he said, "so far as I know I haven't a trace of Jewish blood in me. I wish I had a little. But I'm straight Dutch and Irish." And he sang his favorite song: "The Irish, the Irish, they don't amount to much, but they're a damned sight better than the Goddamned Dutch." (*Remembers*, 34)

But Dunne's Mr. Dooley saw the newspapers themselves as profoundly democratic and also functioning as the great levelers of social custom: "A gr-reat panorama iv life is th' daily press. Here ye can meet kings, imp'rors, an' prisidints, murdhrers, scientists, highway robbers, an' s'ciety leaders; watch dynasties tumble an' heavyweight champeens; see gr-reat cities rocked be earthquakes an' larn to tak th' knife be th' handle, not th' blade whin 'atin' spinach" (*Liberty*, April 10, 1926, 35–38).

Another aspect of Dooley's reductionism—juxtaposition— develops naturally from newspapers, as in the example of earthquakes set beside table manners. Often startling and ironic as well as humorous, it may be observed, perhaps too conveniently, when the politician confronts his public and when Bryan's oratory may be recognized as hot air: "D'ye mind th' time we wint down to th' Coleesyum an' he come out in a black alapaca coat an' pushed into th' air th' finest wurruds ye iver heerd spoke in all ye'er bor-rn days? 'Twas a balloon ascinsion an' th' las' days iv Pompey an' a blast on th' canal all in wan. I had

to hold on to me chair to keep fr'm goin' up in th' air"
(*Philosophy*, 209). Often another face of democracy, juxtaposition in numerous examples puts the sophisticated to bed with the
mundane and moves the farflung palace to humble Archey Road.

Dooley frequently made himself and his own the butt of his
jokes, as in his reaction to the candidacy of Admiral Dewey:
"Manny iv me rilitives has been candydates, but they niver cud
win out again th' r-rest iv th' fam'ly." At his most memorable,
Dooley becomes epigrammatic: "He'll find that a man can be
r-right an' be prisidint, but he can't be both at th' same time"
(*Philosophy*, 175–80). And regardless of debates whether Dooley
(or Dunne) is Irish in authenticity or in pose, an encounter with
an Irish expression no doubt settles the argument for many
readers; "Divvle a wurrud have I to say again' Thomas
[Jefferson]" says Mr. Dooley, and gives his word ("He was a
good man in his day, though I don't know that his battin' av'rage
'd be high again' th' pitchin' iv these times") a special charm (see
Philosophy, 212). Though the dialect has waned in the second
half of the twentieth century, the reader who stays with two or
three essays generally has no problem thereafter. Franklin P.
Adams saw the use of dialect a necessity for the expression of
Dunne's social consciousness, as he explains that

the "Dooley" sketches would never have been printed unless they had
been written in dialect. For editors, fearful of calling names, feel that
the advertisers and the politicians and the social leaders—money,
politics, and social ambition being the Achilles heels of editors and
publishers—are journalism's sacred cows. But if pretense and hypocrisy
are attacked by the office clown, especially in dialect, the crooks and
the shammers think that it is All in Fun. (*At His Best*, xvii)

Assisting Dooley in extending his vistas were a cast of
neighborhood characters modestly representing the world:
Father Kelly to unite practicality and metaphysics, Dock
O'Leary to contrast the old and the new medicine; Molly
Donahue to present the feminist view; Hogan to be his
everyman; Hip Lung as Chinaman; Schwartzmeister, another
pub owner, to initiate a discussion and to assist in its conclusion.
Most frequently the person acts as straight man, as in the
conclusion of "Alcohol as Food": " 'Dy'e think ye-ersilf it sustains
life?' asked Mr. Hennessy. 'It has sustained mine fr many years,'

said Mr. Dooley" (*Philosophy*, 153). But Hennessy more frequently functions to moderate the malice and the cynicism. When, for example, Dooley sees himself and America overwhelmed by "four hundherd millyons of Chinese," Hennessy scolds him and cuts short his rhetoric: " 'End ye'r blather,' said Mr. Hennessy. 'They won't be anny Chinymen left whin Imp'ror Willum gets through' " (*Philosophy*, 82).

Contrary to the cult of ignorance, the *seeming* ignorant often conveys devastating humor; and in that respect Hennessy functions at his best. Although Dooley in "Oratory" told about his own failures in public speaking (*Dissertations*, 19-26), political oratory as sham proved a recurrent Dooley topic (see "On Oratory in Politics" with William J. O'Brien in *Peace*, 218-22 and Senator Albert Beveridge on the Philippines in "Young Oratory" in *Philosophy*, 129-33). Of all famous speeches, however, one stood out. It would seem that, in the late 1890s, every alert citizen could quote the conclusion of the speech by which William Jennings Bryan secured the 1896 Democratic party nomination. Of the speech itself, Harry Thurston Peck wrote, "Twenty thousand men and women went mad with an irresistible enthusiasm . . . he had played at will upon their very heartstrings, until the full tide of their emotion was let loose in one tempestuous roar of passion, which seemed to have no end."[16] No one could forget Bryan's last sentence: "You shall not press down upon the brow of labor this crown of thorns, you shall not crucify mankind upon a cross of gold." Least of all would the inimitable Dooley forget those words, or seek to interrupt himself except for effect. Yet Hennessy brilliantly falls into his act as if the part had been written for him as Dooley recites his version of Bryan's speech:

"Whin I see th' face iv that man who looks like a two-dollar pitcher iv Napolyeon at Saint Heleena," he says, "I say to mesilf, ye shall not—ye shall not—what th' divvle is it ye shall not do, Hinnissy?"

"Ye shall not crucify mankind upon a crown iv thorns," said Mr. Hennessy.

"Right ye ar-re, I forgot," Mr. Dooley went on. "Well, thim were his own wurruds . . . he made th' whole iv th' piece out iv his own head." (*Philosophy*, 210)

Hennessy generally exhibits sufficient skill in recognition and recollection of the events of the world, as in the introduction to this same piece, when he remarks that Bryan is "th' grandest talker that's lived since Dan'l O'Connell." Occasionally he punctures the balloon of Dooley's hyperbole, as in the example of Dooley's exposition of the virtues of a bachelor's life, and strikes a sore spot:

"Sure I have th' finest fam'ly in th' city. Without scandal I'm th' father iv ivry child in Ar-rchey r-road fr'm end to end."
   "An' none iv ye'er own," said Mr. Hennessy.
   "I wish to hell, Hinnissy," said Mr. Dooley savagely, "ye'd not lean against that mirror, I don't want to have to tell ye again." (*Philosophy*, 241)

Although the essays offer mainly Dooley monologues, Hennessy's role deserves study; he makes them dialogues.

   To assess the quality of Finley Peter Dunne's humor means to place his work in the context of the art and its history—surely more than a book-length study. Philip Dunne expressed the desire that his father's position be traced out "in the main line of American humor, in particular political satire, from Petroleum V. Nasby, Artemus Ward, Orpheus C. Kerr, Mark Twain, George Ade, Ring Lardner etc. to such modern-day practitioners as Art Buchwald and Mort Sahl." Surely Dunne's brilliance equals that of H. L. Mencken; but with the moderating presence of Hennessy and his own desire not to commit harm in the name of fun (he deleted some passages when preparing the essays for books), the Dooley essays scarcely convey abiding contempt or rancor, and they do not attempt reform as do, perhaps, the comments of Mort Sahl. President Roosevelt responded fervently to Dunne's essay on the Anglo-Saxon and added, "You may think I have taken your article rather seriously, and so I have, because I think you are a force that counts and I do not want to see you count on the side of certain ugly and unpleasant tendencies in American life."[17] The same sense of force may account for the reaction of President John F. Kennedy when Mort Sahl attempted a joke: ' "I said, I have a bulletin. Marilyn Monroe is going to marry Adlai Stevenson. Now, Kennedy can be jealous of him twice.' And I heard a fist come down on the table, and a voice in a New England dialect saying 'Goddam it.' " Dunne was not refused work, as Mort Sahl reports he was,[18] on the basis of his humor.

Philip Dunne's letter continues, "Will Rogers' on-stage act was an amalgam of Dooley-style comment and of private performances by Bill's friend, the painter Charlie Russell, who used to do monologues with rope tricks. (I knew Rogers well in the early 30's, and he confirmed to me that those were his sources.)"[19] Certainly Will Rogers's use of the newspapers was similar to that of Mr. Dooley's: "I see the South American countries are comin' into the war," and other similar beginnings marked his reliance on them. Rogers's nephew Bruce Quisenberry tells about his techniques: "When we would get to the town, he would go to see some person he knew. If he didn't know anybody, he would go to the newspaper and get what he called 'the dope.' " Writing names on the backs of envelopes, he would consult the notes before he went on stage.[20] His biographer, Homer Croy, reports his attempts at Mr. Dooley imitation,[21] but perhaps Rogers worked his best effort for Mr. Dooley when a woman purist accused him of violating the laws of syntax. " 'Syntax?' he repeated, trying to think his way through a word which plainly was a stranger. 'It must be bad, havin' both sin and tax in it.' "[22]

Doubtless there is no shortage of humorists with whom Dunne may be compared, yet the simplest approach is to show how Dunne's work remains distinctive, how unlike any of the others it is. Its scope, furthermore, offers something to please almost anyone. To the Irish, or the Irish-American, it seems peculiarly Irish; to the unethnic or amalgamated American, it seems particularly American, especially in its extrapolation from current history and politics; in its scaffold of simplicity it may recall "Lum an' Abner" of radio fame; for its brevity, Charles Schulz, since Lucy's "my head is dead," for example, makes the human anatomy an encumbrance as did Dooley's having his feet towed; for its sophistication, wit and wisdom, the analyses of "Wit and Its Relation to the Unconscious" written by Sigmund Freud. But Dunne characterized his own humor best when he recognized the pervasiveness of wisdom and the depth of intelligence when he had Dooley remark of the people of Archey Road, "Simple, says ye! Simple like th' air or th' deep sea."

CHAPTER 4

Mr. Dooley on War and Wars

WHILE the Dooley essays were beginning to attract national attention in 1898, with Boston and Buffalo the first cities outside Chicago to publish them, the Spanish-American War, as Elmer Ellis said, "led to a series [by Dunne] that swept the country like a prairie fire."[1] During the war, two New York newspapers, the *World* of Joseph Pulitzer (with the *Chicago Tribune* an affiliate) and the *Journal* of William Randolph Hearst engaged in a struggle for supremacy. With Spanish censorship of news from Cuba, news was smuggled to Key West and sent from there by telegraph. For the average reader, Mr. Dooley had the rare talent of turning to good use an unpopular or embarrassing incident that had been exploited by the newspapers; his was a voice of moderation, consistently accurate, for he did not deny the faults of those persons and forces he defended. For the scholar, his work had the authenticity which led John Chamberlain some years later to say, "Certainly a dandy course in pre-war [World War I] American history could be taught by taking Mr. Dooley as a three-times-a-week plain English text."[2]

To introduce Spanish and American differences, Dunne placed first in *Mr. Dooley in Peace and in War* (1898) his essay "On Diplomacy." The essay had its origins in the character of President William McKinley (1843–1901), of whom the contemporary historian Gerald F. Linderman writes, "Few presidents have surpassed the social distance William McKinley traveled between impecunious, semirural origins and the White House."[3] In the background of the essay, also, is a letter defaming McKinley written by Dupuy De Lome, the Spanish Minister to Washington to Jose Canalejas y Mendez, editor of *El Heraldo de Madrid*, who was at the time of writing in Havana. It was stolen and published in the *New York Journal* (February 9, 1898), and stated in part,

Besides the natural and inevitable coarseness with which he [McKinley] repeats all that the press and public opinion of Spain has said of [Valeriano] Weyler [Spanish commander in Cuba], it shows once more that McKinley is—weak and catering to the rabble, and, besides, a low politician, who desires to leave a door open to me and to stand well with the jingoes of his part.[4]

Without referring to the incident, Mr. Dooley posed the problem of the sophistication of the Spanish prime minister, Praxedes Sagasta, in comparison with William McKinley. Dooley saw in Sagasta a person who "F'r years an' years [has] played on'y profissionals. . . . He's been up again Gladstun an' Bisma'arck an' ol' what-ye-call-'im, th' Eyetalian,—his name's got away from me,—an' he's done thim all." By heaping encomiums of a contrasting nature upon his friend Mack, Mr. Dooley revealed the president's newly acquired competence in negotiating his physical surroundings:

Oh, but he's a proud man. He's been in town long enough f'r to get out iv th' way iv th' throlley ca'ar whin the bell rings. He's larned not to thry an' light his see-gar at th' ilicthric light. He doesn't offer to pay th' ilivator ma'an f'r carryin' him upstairs. He's got so he can pass a tall buildin' without thryin' f'r to turn a back summersault. An' he's as haughty about it as a new man on an icewagon. (*Peace*, 1–5)

McKinley prayed regularly and saluted his wife at the same hour each day from the White House office, but, said Mr. Dooley, "whin it comes to di-plomacy, th' Spanyard has him again th' rail, an' counts on him till his ar-m is sore." Linderman writes that McKinley "lived in the White House exactly as . . . in Canton, Ohio," and was "so much the model 'Christian Statesman' that the very consistency of his behavior verged on parody of a stock figure" (*Mirror of War*, 22). Nevertheless, Dooley resolved the conflict to McKinley's credit by positing a comparison with two of his friends who attended the annual picnic at Ogden's grove, "where wanst a year Ireland's freed," and lost their money in a shell game. Alluding to McKinley's delay in reaching a decision about the war (see *Mirror of War*, 31–34), Dooley said, "It took O'Brien some time f'r to decide what to do. Thin says he, ' 'Twas my money this fool blowed in.' An' he made a dash f'r th' shell ma-an; an' he not on'y got what he'd lost, but all th' r-rest iv th' capital besides. Ye see, that was his game. That was where he come in" (*Peace*, 1–5).

I *The Spanish-American War*

The implied punch at Spain was delayed in delivery, but late in April 1898, after war was declared, Congress voted an increase of the regular army to 62,597 men and the raising of a volunteer army of 125,000 men. The additional authorization for the president to accept directly three regiments of volunteer cavalry enabled Theodore Roosevelt, then Assistant Secretary of the Navy, to lead a regiment; though he was without battle experience, he modestly accepted a lieutenant-colonelcy.

So eager were Americans to join in this war that a call for 30,000 volunteers yielded responses of around 1 million. Linderman writes, "Indeed, there were 30,000 pertinacious applicants for general and general staff officer positions alone" (*Mirror of War*, 62). The volunteers, however, as well as their relatives and friends, saw no necessity to succumb to the rigors of military detachment; Russell A. Alger, the Secretary for War, wrote into his account of the war the example of the young woman who requested that the sailing of the fleet be delayed two days because, otherwise, a birthday box sent her brother would not reach him before embarkation.[5] General Nelson A. Miles, age sixty-two, had experience, but most of it irrelevant because it had been gained in the Civil War and Indian War, and was now grown accustomed to easy life. Each official sought his own means, based on private preferences rather than military strategy, to defeat the Spanish.

These three factors Dooley combined in his speech "On War Preparations." Mr. Hennessy inquires whether the army has started for Cuba yet, and Mr. Dooley begins his account with "Wan ar-rmy, says ye? Twinty!"—among which "th' reg'lar cavalry, con-sistin' iv four hundherd an' eight thousan' well-mounted men . . . departed on their earned [errand] iv death amidst th' cheers iv eight millyon sojers left behind at Chickamaha." General Miles arrived with "his intire fam'ly with him," and among the various cabinet members with their several strategies, "I've heerd that th' President is arrangin' a knee dhrill, with th' idee iv prayin' th' villyans to th' divvil." But with all, says Mr. Dooley, General Miles plans to destroy the Spanish with one blow (*Peace*, 6–9).

What Roosevelt accomplished by way of congressional

authorization for his volunteer cavalry provides some insight into the use of personal power rather than military qualifications in gaining appointments. Said Mr. Dooley in an essay called "On Some Army Appointments," "We go into this war, if we iver do go into it, with th' most fash'nable ar-rmy that iver creased its pants. 'Twil be a daily hint fr'm Paris to th' crool foe" (*Peace*, 25-29).

Despite a fleet of journalists in the field, communications became a major block to intelligent decision making. In fact, the War Department had made no provisions for news from the front and often was embarrassed to receive news as citizens did—from the newspapers. Lack of communications was combined with the general ineptitude of the persons making the decisions.

The president's strategy council on April 29 ordered General Shafter to land 5,000 troops on the south coast of Cuba, but in the brief interval between their making the decision and issuing the order, Admiral Cervera sailed west from the Cape Verde Islands, possibly—they could not tell for sure—to relieve Havana; the order was canceled on April 30. Another plan, for Shafter to take 12,000 troops to Key West, was originated on May 2 and canceled a few days later; there was not sufficient fresh water at Key West for sustaining a body of troops. Of the 15,000 men awaiting embarkation from Tampa, only 5,000 could be accommodated, although another thousand squeezed in. Also, after Roosevelt succeeded in blocking a gangway except to access of his Rough Riders, his triumph was marred because their horses must be left behind. On receiving orders from Washington on June 7 that "the President directs you to sail at once with what force you have ready," Shafter announced a June 8 departure; but a telegram came from Washington canceling the expedition because word had been received that the Spanish ships were not where they were thought to be in Santiago Harbor. The men stayed on board, sweltering in tropical sun, until June 14, when they put to sea.

These are only a few of the instructions commanded and countermanded, in response to which Dunne wrote "On Strategy." The essay pictures the president's strategy board enjoying a game of checkers. "Insthruct Schley to put on all steam, an' thin put it off again, an' call us up be telephone. R-rush eighty-three millyon throops an' four mules to Tampa, to Mobile, to Chickenmaha, to Coney Island, to Ireland, to th' divvle, an' r-rush thim back again. Don't r-rush thim. Ordher Sampson to pick up th' cable at Lincoln Par-rk, an' run into th' bar-rn. Is th' balloon corpse r-ready? It is? Thin don't sind it up. Sind it up," and so the sequence of contradictions continues. Dooley was not to forget the plush surroundings of Tampa, which officers and press corps enjoyed and which Charles H. Brown described in a chapter headed "Piazza Pieces at Tampa." Brown quotes from the report of George Kennan: "Two regimental bands were playing waltzes and patriotic airs under a long row of incandescent lights on the broad veranda . . . the rotunda was crowded with officers, war correspondents, and gaily attired ladies, and the impression made upon a newcomer, as he alighted from the train, was that of a brilliant military ball at a fashionable seaside summer resort."[6] Mr. Dooley adds, "Teddy Rosenfelt's r-rough r-riders ar-re downstairs, havin' their uniforms pressed. Ordher thim to th' goluf links at wanst" (*Peace*, 30–33).

Those same frustrations Dunne wrote into "On Mules and Others," in which, before its end, it is difficult to tell which army leaders are the mules and which the jackasses. "The Alger gyards" is a group of "gallant mules . . . led be a most courageous jackass," who attack the camp at Tampa. The leaders are "as efficient a lot iv mules as iver exposed their ears. Th' trouble is with th' rank an' file," Mr. Dooley asserts. "They're men. What's needed to carry on this war as it goes to-day is an ar-rmy iv jacks an' mules. Whin ye say to a man, 'Git ap, whoa, gee, back up, get alang!' he don't know what ye'er dhrivin' at or to. But a mule hears th' ordhers with a melancholy smile, drhoops his ears, an' follows his war-rm, moist breath. Th' ordhers fr'm Washin'ton is perfectly comprehinsible to a jackass, but they don't mane annything to a poor, foolish man. No human bein', Hinnissy, can undherstand what the divvle use it was to sink a ship that cost two hundherd thousan' dollars an' was worth at laste eighty dollars in Sandago Harbor, if we have to keep fourteen ships outside to prevint five Spanish ships f'rm sailin'." And further examples follow (*Peace*, 14–19).

Before the war, Spanish mistreatment of American citizens in Cuba so enraged the public that when General Fitzhugh Lee took command of the consul-general's office in Havana on June 3, 1896, there was, as Henry Cabot Lodge wrote, a popular confidence that his "good sense and firm courage"[7] would earn just treatment of American prisoners. Mr. Dooley reflected this feeling in "On Fitz-Hugh Lee," whom he was proud to claim as a possible relative because "Th' Fitz-Hughs an' th' McHughs an' th' McKeoughs is not far apart. I have a cousin be th' name iv McKeough." That strong measures were necessary appeared in Dooley's praise of General Lee's imposing physical appearance ("A fat ma-an, with a head like a football an' a neck big enough to pump blood into his brain an' keep it fr'm starvin' ") and in his certain temper: "whin his face flames an' his neck swells an' his eyes look like a couple iv illicthric lamps again a cyclone sky, he'd lead a forlorn hope acrost th' battlemints iv hell." General Lee's reports were a major feature of the war news, and it was he who requested that the *Maine* be sent to Cuba (*Peace,* 10–13). When the events were over, Dunne wrote "On the Destruction of Cervera's Fleet," an essay which Elmer Ellis calls "the piece that made Mr. Dooley a national hero almost overnight." Into this piece Dunne packed an astounding number and variety of details of attitudes (at home and at war) and colorful events of a complex history. The details he selected, briefly retold below, demonstrates the information (not ignorance) on which Dunne based the essays which made him famous; the essay itself follows for convenient study of his techniques.

II   *The Factual Bases for a Popular Essay*

In the background of Dunne's essay is the *Maine's* occupation of Havana harbor with the avowed purpose of a friendly naval visit to relieve tension between Spain and the United States. The *New York Times* had bragged of that vessel's indestructibility in declaring that its armor belt "insures immunity against heavy projectiles making an opening where the water can rush in";[8] but on February 15, 1898, the *Maine* exploded and sank with the loss of two officers and 258 men. Although a Court of Inquiry was ordered, the newspapers—without waiting for findings of accident or intention—demanded immediate retaliatory action. The Hearst papers originated a slogan, "Remember the *Maine* and to hell with Spain!" War was officially declared April 21, but in the meantime Congress had to provide a navy on short notice against a country which, along with other European nations, could be expected to have at hand some high-powered torpedo craft. Fortunately in 1890 Congress had authorized construction of three battleships, the *Indiana,* the *Massachusetts,* and the *Oregon;* two years later the *Iowa* was authorized and with the *Texas* and *Brooklyn* of earlier vintage made a total of six battleships to be employed against Spain. But now Congress scurried about to buy or to lease steamers, yachts, and transports which could be converted to gunboats. In this effort, the navy commandeered the yacht *Corsair II,* belonging to John Pierpont Morgan and commissioned it the U.S.S. *Gloucester.*

Admiral Cervera sailed from the Azores and arrived in Martinique on May 11, but in the midst of war hysteria his "powerful squadron" was reported off New York, Providence, Boston, and Washington. H. Wayne Morgan writes, "Hysterical state governors and local defense committees envisioned shots falling in the streets of a hundred towns, as if the Spanish Navy covered the whole Atlantic."[9] The war was farther away, however, in Cuba, where General William Shafter planned an attack on July 1 near Santiago. Subsequently, the success of the famed battle of "San Juan Hill" (actually Kettle Hill in the San Juan group) which vaulted Theodore Roosevelt and his Rough Riders into fame (July 1 and 2) enabled the United States on July 3 to threaten a July 4 bombardment of the city. With Cervera's fleet "bottled up" in the harbor, the army was to march on Santiago. Richard Harding Davis, an American correspondent with the army, remarked that this was "probably the only instance when an army was called upon to capture a fleet" (*Fate,* 144).

On the morning of July 3, Admiral William T. Sampson in his flagship the *New York* left the fleet in Santiago harbor to confer with General Shafter at Siboney, eleven miles east of Santiago, about a combined army-navy operation. Sampson was supreme commander of the North Atlantic Squadron, or, as he was alternately called, commander of the East-West Squadrons, a farflung title which enabled Mr. Dooley to exaggerate Sampson's position as near Cadiz and the Suez Canal. As Sampson steamed away, he left behind, blockading the harbor, the East Squadron, still technically under his command, and the West Squadron under Commodore Winfield Schley on the *Brooklyn.* The *Massachusetts* had earlier departed from the blockading line bound for coal; remaining in the blockade were the battleships *Indiana, Oregon, Iowa, Texas,* and *Brooklyn,* and the two armed yachts, the *Vixen* and the *Gloucester.*

Cervera, who had predicted an American victory, had already evidenced that the otherwise-villified Spaniards could be gentlemen. Shortly before, when an American crew of eight volunteers maneuvered the old collier the *Merrimac* into the channel and sank it—though not in the proper spot—in an attempt to blockade Cervera's fleet, Cervera took the men prisoners but courteously informed Admiral Sampson that the crew of the *Merrimac* were safe. Caught in the blockade, Cervera was aboard the flagship the *Infanta Maria Teresa* with three other armored cruisers under his command: the *Vizcaya,* the *Cristobal Colon,* and the *Almirante Oquendo.* Also he commanded two destroyers, the *Pluton* and the *Furor.* Some of his men, as well as Finley Peter Dunne, were aware of Castilian dignity. The captain of the *Teresa* said, "My bugles were the last echo of those that history tells were sounded in the taking of Granada. It was the signal that the history of four centuries of greatness was ended, and that Spain had passed into a nation of the fourth class" (*Fate,* 149).

Yet at the time Cervera began a futile run for freedom, supplies were so low that, in the words of Mr. Dooley, only the armor plate and the bed ticks remained to be eaten. The crew of the *Colon* had been without food for twenty-four hours and could fight only briefly on the strength of brandy; earlier their crew had mutinied, some sailors had been shot, and with evident poor morale they surrendered without a fight.

At 9:30 on the morning of July 3, Cervera's squadron began to move out; at 9:31 a lookout on the *Iowa* spotted the movement, gave a shout, and the gun crew fired a warning shot. The signalman hoisted No. 250, "The enemy's ships are escaping." Immediately the *Oregon* also fired, sounded its siren, and hoisted the signal. "On the *Iowa,*" writes historian John Edward Weems, "Seaman Mike Flynn hurried to a forward six-inch gun, and Apprentice Alonzo Willis ran to a six-inch gun aft on the port side. Both men happily contemplated the chance for revenge for the *Maine*" (*Fate,* 148). The same general feeling prompted cheers as men ran to their stations; but Mr. Dooley's account of the playing of the national anthem comes from at least two sources. An incident had occurred in the earlier history of the *Maine* when, on July 29, 1897, Captain Charles Sigsbee was caught in collision circumstances in the East River with three steamers, two of them excursion ships, and a barge. The band aboard the excursion steamer *Isabel* struck up "The Star-Spangled Banner" to quiet the panic; but Sigsbee rammed the pier instead of the *Isabel*, and the *Maine* sustained only minor damage. Now, with the naval battle in progress at Santiago de Cuba, Captain John Philip of the *Texas* felt constrained to admonish the jubilant crew: "Don't cheer, boys. The poor devils are dying" (*Fate*, 152). But on July 3, as Alger wrote, the troops in the rifle-pits also cheered and danced and embraced each other. General Shafter cabled, "A regimental band that had managed to keep its instruments on the line played 'The Star-Spangled Banner' and 'There will be a hot time in the old town to-night.' "[10]

His flagship blazing, Cervera ordered it shoreward, where it grounded at a cove six and one-half miles from the harbor. When lowered boats sank, the officers and crew were forced to leap into the water, many with their clothes aflame. Cervera himself, nearly naked, was lifted from the water by the crew of the *Gloucester*. The "converted yacht" had helped to destroy the Spanish *Pluton* and had sunk the *Furor*.

From having signaled Cervera's attempt at escape, the *Iowa* remained consistently in the battle, firing steadily from 9:40 when Commodore Schley ordered the guns of the *Brooklyn*, the *Texas*, the *Iowa*, and the *Indiana* into action against the *Teresa*. With the *Teresa* and the *Oquendo* destroyed, the Americans on the *Brooklyn, Oregon, Texas*, and *Iowa* turned their fire on the *Vizcaya*. Admiral Sampson had turned the *New York* back toward the harbor and, after the *Indiana* had been ordered returned to its blockading station, signaled Captain Robley Evans of the *Iowa* also to return. The *Iowa* stopped to pick up survivors from the *Vizcaya*. When the last Spanish ship, the mutinied *Colon*, ran up a white flag, the battle ended at 1:15 P.M.

Finley Peter Dunne capitalized on the tendency of officers after an unprepared-for and unplanned battle to congratulate themselves. Sampson, who was steaming away from the fight and on return fired only three four-inch shells at the *Furor*, in his report gave no credit to Schley, who was in the fight throughout. However, the main action of the *Brooklyn*, Schley's ship, consisted of following the *Oregon*'s example in firing a shot which persuaded the *Colon* to turn toward land and surrender (though the shots of neither ship reached the *Colon*). The *Oregon* had thirteen-inch guns, the *Brooklyn* eight-inch guns.

Though sentiments to this day vary, the author of the *Encyclopaedia Britannica* version simply states, "When the *Oregon* had fired five shells, the *Colon* hauled down her colours." In view of this, Schley's telegram sent to Captain Charles Clark of the *Oregon* seems somewhat begrudging: "Congratulations on the grand victory. Thanks for spendid assistance." Schley's official report of the battle, sent to Sampson as his commanding officer, included the observation, "The victory seems big enough for all of us" (*Fate*, 155). But Sampson's first report to the Secretary of the Navy failed to mention Commodore Schley.

These bits of egotism no doubt inspired Dunne's self-congratulatory telegrams from William McKinley, James Wilson, and Russell Alger. But perhaps the most outrageous of Dunne's witticisms is that about the beginning of the battle: "Admiral Sampson was settin' playin' sivin up with Admiral Schley." It confirms, as Secretary of the Navy John D. Long wrote, that "neither of them was an essential factor in the immediate fighting."[11] Dooley's statement mischievously implies, moreover, that these two rivals were close friends. The "bitter controversy" which arose after the battle, however, occurred between friends of Schley and Sampson about the respective credits bestowed on either. To reward the two officers, the Navy Department advanced Sampson eight numbers in grade but Schley only six numbers. A Court of Inquiry was not ordered until two years later, when Admiral Schley requested it to resolve the antagonism. On July 3, 1899, John D. Long sent a letter to President McKinley with regard to the alleged "Persecution of Admiral Schley." What came out as the controversy raged is summarized in President Roosevelt's reply on February 18, 1902: "the majority of these actions which the court censures occurred five weeks or more before the fight itself; and it certainly seems that if Admiral Schley's actions were censurable he should not have been left as second in command under Admiral Sampson. His offenses were in effect condoned when he was not called to account for them. Admiral Sampson, after the fight, in an official letter to the department, alluded for the first time to Admiral Schley's 'reprehensible conduct' six weeks previously" (Appendix B, *Navy*, 196).

Dunne's Mr. Dooley sums up the action: "This is a gr-reat day f'r Ioway." This double entendre refers to the battleship *Iowa* and to James Wilson as Secretary of Agriculture. Wilson

(1836-1920) was a Scotsman who came to the United States in 1851 and settled in Tama County, Iowa, in 1855. He represented his county in the Twelfth General Assembly of Iowa, and in the fall of 1872 he was elected to Congress from the fifth district. From Congress he retired to his farm and formed a syndicate of daily newspapers, for which he contributed a column about farming; no doubt this was known to fellow-journalist Finley Peter Dunne. Later Wilson became professor of agriculture at the State Agricultural College at Ames and director of the experiment station, where President McKinley discovered him in 1897, when Wilson was sixty-two years old, and effected the beginning of a new career for him. Succeeding presidents Roosevelt and Taft kept Wilson in the cabinet until 1913, which means that he retired from public life at the age of seventy-eight. While Secretary of Agriculture, he endowed the position with new dignity and made the department a source of vital information. The Iowa historian Johnson Brigham perhaps caught the same element Dunne discerned when he wrote, "It was a proverb in Washington that when the President was in doubt he called in the canny Scotchman."[12] Today in Washington, D.C., the Agricultural Building with twin arches across Independence Avenue commemorates the work of James Wilson. The other sender of a Dooley-type telegram, Russell A. Alger, was Secretary of War, 1897-1899, and published *Spanish-American War* (1900); he resigned at President McKinley's request because of criticism of his department's inefficiency, especially in handling the return of the troops. Dunne's telegrams, also, parody the messages written by Chauncey Depew, then United States Senator, congratulating McKinley.

Although as Dunne conceived and developed his two characters. Mr. Hennessy's wit was intentionally surpassed by that of his elder, Mr. Hennessy was capable of satire and of puns, as in the example of his comment on George Dixon, the world's bantamweight champion, 1890-1892. The "Admiral Cervera" piece, in one sentence by Mr. Hennessy, provides actually a triple entendre because George William Dixon was active in Chicago business, civic, and social affairs, and served as Methodist superintendent of Sunday School for thirty-eight years. Of remaining details, Jose Manuel Pando was a Bolivian revolutionary who, shortly after this essay was written, became president of Bolivia (1899-1904), but scarcely aided the naval battle at

Santiago. The newspaper in What Cheer, Iowa, was the *Patriot Chronicle*. The dispatch boats of the newspapers (or press boats, as they were called) played a significant role in what Charles H. Brown called "the correspondents' war." He reports George Kennan's conversation with Admiral Sampson on the flagship, when the deck officer bluntly repeated the Admiral's warning: "If you show up at night in the neighborhood of this ship, we shall fire on you first and ask questions afterward." He observed several press boats racing to Key West and the cable office to "be first with the news of the approach of Commodore Schley's Flying Squadron . . . all blowing their whistles vigorously to attract attention from the shore" (*Correspondents*, 168).

Selecting these details from current events, Dunne created a Dooley-Hennessy conversation inspired by a combination of characteristic journalistic inaccuracy and a temporary strike of the stereotypers which, as an inserted epigraph in *Mr. Dooley in Peace and in War* informs its readers, "caused the English newspapers of Chicago temporarily to suspend publication," actually from July 1 to 6, at the climax of the war. The essay follows, with Hennessy beginning by punning on Chicago reading fare:

"Th' What Cheer, Iowa, Lamp iv Freedom is on th' streets with a tillygram that Shafter has captured Sandago de Cuba, an' is now settin' on Gin'ral Pando's chest with his hands in his hair. But this is denied be th' Palo Gazoot, the Macoupin County Raygisther, an' th' Meridyan Sthreet Afro-American. I also see be th' Daily Scoor Card, th' Wine List, th' Deef Mute's Spokesman, th' Morgue Life, the Bill iv Fare, th' Stock Yards Sthraight Steer, an' Jack's Tips on th' Races, th' on'y daily paper printed in Chicago, that Sampson's fleet is in th' Suez Canal bombarding Cades. Th' Northwestern Christyan Advycate says this is not thru, but that George Dixon was outpointed by an English boxer in a twinty-r-round go in New York."

"Ye've got things mixed up," said Mr. Dooley. "I get th' news sthraight. 'Twas this way. Th' Spanish fleet was bottled up in Sandago Harbor, an' they dhrew th' cork. That's a joke. I see it in th pa-apers. Th' gallant boys iv th' navy was settin' out on th' deck, defindin' their counthry an' dhrawin' three ca-ards apiece, whin th' Spanish admiral con-cluded 'twud be better f'r him to be desthroyed on th' ragin' sea, him bein' a sailor, thin to have to have his fleet captured be cav'lry. Annyhow, he was willin' to take a chance; an' he says to his sailors: 'Spanyards,' he says, 'Castiles,' he says, 'we have et th' las' bed-tick,' he says; 'an', if we stay here much longer,' he says, 'I'll have to have a steak

off th' armor plate fried f'r ye,' he says. 'Lave us go out where we can
have a r-run f'r our money,' he says. An' away they wint. I'll say this
much f'r him, he's a brave man, a dam brave man. I don't like a
Spanyard no more than ye do, Hinnissy. I niver see wan. But, if this here
man was a—was a Zulu, I'd say he was a brave man. If I was aboord wan
iv thim yachts that was converted, I'd go to this here Cervera, an' I'd
say: 'Manuel,' I'd say, 'ye're all-right, me boy. Ye ought to go to a doctor
an' have ye'er eyes re-set, but ye're a good fellow. Go downstairs,' I'd
say, 'into th' basemint iv the ship,' I'd say, 'an' open th' cupboard jus'
nex' to th' head iv th' bed, an' find th' bottle marked "Floridy Wather,"
an' threat ye'ersilf kindly.' That's what I'd say to Cervera. He's all right.

"Well, whin our boys see th' Spanish fleet comin' out iv th' harbor,
they gathered on th' deck an' sang th' naytional anthem, 'They'll be a
hot time in th' ol' town tonight.' A lift-nant come up to where Admiral
Sampson was settin' playin' sivin up with Admiral Schley. 'Bill,' he says,
'th' Spanish fleet is comin' out,' he says. 'What talk have ye?' says
Sampson. 'Sind out some row-boats an' a yacht, an' desthroy thim. Clubs
is thrumps,' he says, and he wint on playin'. Th' Spanish fleet was
attackted on all sides be our br-rave la-ads, nobly assisted be th'
dispatch boats iv the newspapers. Wan by wan they was desthroyed.
Three battleships attackted th' converted yacht Gloucester. Th'
Gloucester used to be owned be Pierpont Morgan; but 'twas converted,
an' is now leadin' a dacint life. Th' Gloucester sunk thim all, th'
Christobell Comma, the Viscera, an' th' Admiral O'Quinn. It thin wint
up to two Spanish torpedo boats an' giv thim wan punch, an' away they
wint. Be this time th' sojers had heerd of the victhry, an' they gathered
on th' shore, singin' the naytional anthem, 'They'll be a hot time in th'
ol' town to-night, me babby.' Th' gloryous ol' chune, to which
Washington an' Grant an' Lincoln marched, was took up be th' sailors
on th' ships, an' Admiral Cervera r-run wan iv his boats ashore, an'
jumped into th' sea. At last accounts th' followin' dispatches had been
received: 'To Willum McKinley: Congratulations on y'er noble victhry.
(Signed) Willum McKinley.' 'To Russell A. Alger: Ye done splendid.
(Signed) Russell A. Alger.' To James Wilson, Sicrety iv Agriculture: This
is a gr-reat day f'r Ioway. Ar-re ye much hur-rted? (Signed) James
Wilson.' "

"Where did ye hear all this?" asked Mr. Hennessy, in great
amazement.

"I r-read it," said Mr. Dooley, impressively, "in the Staats Zeitung."
(*Peace*, 68–72)

Dunne watched the comedy continue after the cease-fire, when
General Shafter conducted a mail campaign with Spanish
General Toral to persuade him to surrender the city of Santiago,

and negotiations involved a load of hay, which Dunne wrote into "The Hay Fleet" (*Hearts*, 210–15).

III   *Manifesting Our National Character*

Louis Filler called Dunne's designation of Admiral Dewey as his Cousin George "one of his inspired bits of deliberate confusion."[13] " 'Sure,' said Mr. Dooley. 'Dewey or Dooley, 'tis all th' same.' " In December 1897, because of Assistant Secretary of the Navy Roosevelt, George Dewey was given command of the Asiatic Squadron and ordered to the Far East, where he harbored at "Ding Dong" (Hong Kong) until the April 24 British proclamation of neutrality forced him out, whereupon he proceeded to Manila Bay where on May 1 he destroyed the obsolete and poorly defended Spanish ships which their commander, Admiral Montojo, had prudently stationed away from the city. Hailed as a hero by the American public in songs such as "What Did Dewey Do to Them?" and promoted to rear-admiral by the president, Dewey tried to ally the Philippine insurrectionists and tenaciously held out as a German squadron and a British squadron arrived with dubious loyalties. Not until the end of July did General Wesley Merritt arrive to rescue Dewey with a land force of nearly eleven thousand men. Two days after the armistice was signed on August 12, the city of Manila capitulated. On the lack of communication from Dewey, Mr. Dooley said, "He don't care whether we know what he's done or not. I'll bet ye, whin we come to find out about him, we'll hear he's ilicted himself king iv th' F'lip-ine Islands. Dooley th' Wanst" (*Peace*, 20–24). Dooley's was an early dissenting opinion from that of Henry Cabot Lodge, who wrote that Manila "writes the name of George Dewey high up among the greatest of victorious admirals."[14] Of Dewey's extended maneuvers, Dunne wrote "On Admiral Dewey's Activity," in which Mr. Dooley began, "If they don't catch up with him pretty soon, he'll fight his way ar-round th' wurruld, an' come out through Bar-saloona or Cades." Of his fighting a war which was already over, Mr. Dooley declared, "Th' war is not over till Cousin George stops fightin'." He concludes, " 'Tis a tur-ble thing to be a man iv high sperrits, an' not to know whin th' other fellow's licked" (*Peace*, 39–42). In subsequent events, the United States demanded the entirety of the Philippine Islands, an area 7,000 square miles greater than the British Isles. "Wan iv the worst things about this here war is th' way it's making puzzles f'r our poor, tired heads," said Mr. Dooley in "On the Philippines." "I'm askin' mesilf will I annex Cubia or lave it to the Cubians? Will I take Porther Ricky or put it by? An' what shud I do with th' Ph'lippeens? . . . I can't annex thim because I don't know where they ar're. I can't let go iv thim because some wan else'll take thim if I do. They are eight thousan' iv thim islands, with a population iv wan hundherd millyon naked savages; an' me bedroom's crowded now with me an' th' bed" (*Peace,* 43–47).

Such was the operation of Manifest Destiny, in which Dunne could see motives other than piety, despite McKinley's sentiment, after prayer for divine guidance, that "There is nothing left for us to do but to take all the islands and to educate the Filipinos, and uplift, civilize, and Christianize them and, by God's grace, do the very best we can for them as our fellow men, for whom Christ also died."[15] In an essay called "Expansion" in *Mr. Dooley in the Hearts of His Countrymen,* Dunne denounced quite seriously imperialistic threats to conquer a country in the name of freedom: "an' we'll larn ye our language, because 'tis aisier to larn ye ours than to larn oursilves yours. An' we'll give ye clothes, if ye pay f'r thim; an', if ye don't, ye can go without. An' whin ye're hungry, ye can go to th' morgue—we mane th' resth'rant—an' ate a good square meal iv ar-rmy beef." But he concludes, "I don't know what to do with th' Philippeens anny more thin I did las' summer, befure I heerd tell iv thim. We can't give thim to anny wan without makin' th' wan that gets thim feel th' way Doherty felt to Clancy whin Clancy med a frindly call an' give Doherty's childher th' measles. We can't sell thim, we can't ate thim, an' we can't throw thim into th' alley whin no wan is lookin'." He recognizes "Aggynaldoo" (Emilio Aguinaldo) as a leader with his own notions of patriotism and freedom but well understands the imperialist sentiment of the American people who would "give that pathrite what he asks, an' thin they'd throw him down an' taake it away fr'm him" (*Hearts,* 3–7).

In *Mr. Dooley in Peace and in War,* "On General Miles's Moonlight Excursion" marks that occasion when Miles, preferring to let General Shafter maintain the forces in Cuba, requested permission to sail on to Puerto Rico. On July 26 he landed at Guanica, which he found already captured by the

navy, and sailed on to Ponce, which also had been visited by the
Wasp, Annapolis, and *Dixie.* The correspondent Richard Harding Davis described the by now almost comic eagerness of the
natives to surrender to American forces, saying of the city of
Ponce, "It was possessed of the surrender habit in a most
aggravating form." The correspondents wore uniforms, also, and
the natives were prone to surrender to Davis himself. He
continued his report, "as a matter of fact, the town first
surrendered to Ensign Curtin of the *Wasp,* then to three officers
who strayed into it by mistake, then to Commander Davis, and
finally to General Miles" (*Correspondents,* 411). The Puerto
Ricans welcomed the Americans with delirious joy, according to
Chamberlin's account, and with American patriotic music, so that
the conquest earned the name of a "military picnic, a sort of
comic-opera war" (*Correspondents,* 412). This became Mr.
Dooley's "On General Miles's Moonlight Excursion" with its
picnic in "Punch" (Ponce) and its account of General Miles's
acceptance of the advance surrender: "'I congratulate ye,' he
says to the Puerto Ricans, "'on th' heeroism iv yer definse,' he
says. 'Ye stuck manfully to ye colors, whativer they ar-re,' he
says. 'I on'y wondher that ye waited f'r me to come befure
surrindhrin,' he says" (*Peace,* 34–38). After the war, when he told
journalists what he thought of the navy, General Miles incurred
the displeasure of President Roosevelt, a topic Dunne treated in
"White House Discipline" (*Observations,* 57–61).

"On Prayers for Victory" addresses the age-old problem of
two nations praying to the same god for the defeat of the other
and brings out the gallantry and common sense of Father Kelly:

"Hogan," he says, "I'll go into th' battle with a prayer book in wan hand
an' a soord in th' other," he says; "an', if th' wurruk calls f'r two hands,
'tis not th' soord I'll dhrop," he says. "Don't ye believe in prayer?" says
Hogan. "I do," says th' good man; "but," he says, "a healthy person
ought," he says, "to be ashamed," he says, "to ask f'r help in a fight," he
says. (*Peace,* 48–52)

"On a Letter from the Front" attacks the "patriots" at home
who concern themselves chiefly with acquiring wealth and
avoiding the payment of taxes—people such as John D.
Rockefeller, Philip Armour, and John Pierpont Morgan. The
Wilson Bill, proposed in 1888, would have levied an income tax

of 2 percent on incomes over $4,000, but the "sugar senators" and others added 633 amendments and wholly changed the bill. Mr. Dooley scolds the protected interests: "What is it to ye that me nevvew Terry is sleepin' in ditch wather an' atin' hard tacks an' coffee an' bein' r-robbed be leeber [libre] Cubians, an' catchin' yellow fever without a chanst iv givin' it to e'er a Spanyard. Ye think more iv a stamp thin ye do iv ye'er counthry. Ye're like th' Sugar Thrust. F'r two cints ye'd refuse to support th' govermint. I know ye, ye bloated monno-polist." The letter from Mr. Dooley's nephew tells about the rolling mill in Cuba and ends, "Tell me frinds that wan gang iv good la-ads f'rm th' r-road cud wurruk anny three iv th' gangs down here. Th' mills is owned be Rockefellar, so no more at prisint fr'm yer affecshunate nevvew, Peter Casey, who's writin' this f'r me." Objecting to the reported low salaries of Cuban laborers, Mr. Hennessy says, "I don't see how they cud get derrick hands f'r six a week." Mr. Dooley, establishing a common bond between two nations in exploitation, replies, "Me frind Jawn D. knows how" (*Peace*, 58–62).

"On Our Cuban Allies" celebrated two persistent factors in the war: the newspapers' overestimation of Cuban troops, and the differences between American and Cuban cultures, particularly in regard to work. Of the former, Spanish garrisons in Cuba numbered, according to the newspapers, 200,000 men but in actuality about 80,000 men. The other Mr. Dooley phrased as a failure to understand our civilization.

General Calixto Garcia was the insurgent leader who could perhaps support Shafter at Santiago and, prior to that, inform Americans of the location of Spanish fortifications. In the mountains of eastern Cuba, he could not be reached by telegraph, and President McKinley, soon after the outbreak of the war, asked for a man to carry a message. The response of Lieutenant Andrew Summers Rowan (later colonel) became the most famous spy mission of the war and provided the inspiration for Elbert Hubbard's later opinion that he was the real hero of the War. Rowan landed secretly, with only Cuban guards, and, as Hubbard wrote, "in three weeks came out on the other side of the Island."[16] Hubbard's essay, "A Message to Garcia" (1899), sold, by his count, over 40 million copies.

Mr. Dooley calls him "Gin'ral Garshy" and begins by saying Garcia has "with wan hundherd thousan' men's been fightin'

bravely f'r two years f'r to liberyate Cubia." With each reference
the number is reduced, until the close, when "Garshy took his
gallant band iv six back to th' woods; an' there th' three iv thim
ar're now, ar'rmed with forty r-rounds iv canned lobster, an'
ready to raysist to the death." Dooley often referred to the
eagerness of Cubans to raid American supplies, to feast well, but
to offer little help in the war itself. Without the long-range
"acquisitive instinct" of Americans, the Cubans tend to avoid
work and even celebrate being laid off, as Dooley pictures them;
but Americans can still envy the carefree spirit of those who do
not toil against tomorrow. Dooley concludes, "The first thing we
know we'll have another war in Cubia whin we begin dis-
thributin' good jobs, twelve hours a day, wan sivinty-five. Th'
Cubians ain't civilized in our way. I sometimes think I've got a
touch iv Cubian blood in me own veins" (*Peace*, 63–67).

Where Theodore Roosevelt had once written into his diary,
"There is no management whatever in the War Dept.," the worst
was yet to come. Secretary Alger's mishandling of the return of
the troops, mainly because of his fears that they would bring
disease into the country, actually prevented and delayed their
receiving adequate medical care and proper nutrition. There
were 5,000 war dead, but only 379 from battle wounds. When
demands for Alger's resignation increased, Dunne wrote "On a
Letter to Mr. Depew," meaning Chauncey Mitchell Depew
(1834–1928), who had been president of the New York Central
railroad and served as United States Senator (1899–1911). With
rough allusion to Alger's postwar difficulties and General
Sherman's "War is hell" statement, Mr. Dooley says, "He meant
war was hell whin 'twas over." Alger's public acknowledgment of
his at-home sufferings and ignorance of the soldiers' personal
encounters with disease, death, and treachery were duly
observed by Mr. Dooley: "Th' proud an' fearless pathrites who
restrained thimsilves, an' didn't go to th' fr-ront, th' la-ads that
shruggled hard with their warlike tindincies, an' fin'lly downed
thim an' stayed at home an' practised up upon th' typewriter,
they're ragin' an' tearin' an' desthroyin' their foes."

As the essay continues, Alger writes, in naive revelation of his
own inadequacies, to "Chansy Depot," as follows: "In two
months I had enough supplies piled up in Maine to feed ivry sojer
in Cubia." Regarding failure to supply the troops, he says,
"Disgustin' men that've done nawthin' but get thimsilves shot,

ask fr milk an' quinine." His final advice: "Be sicrety of war, if ye
will; but niver be sicrety iv A war" (*Peace*, 73–76).

What happens to a revolutionary leader when his cause fades
into obscurity becomes the subject of Dunne's "A Hero Who
Worked Overtime," for, at the siege of Manila, the Spanish and
American forces joined against Aguinaldo's Filipino guerrillas.
Dooley remarks, "it looks now as if they was nawthin' left fr me
young frind Aggynaldoo to do but time. Like as not a year fr'm
now he'll be in jail, like Napoleon, th' impror iv th' Fr-rinch, was
in his day, an' Mike, th' Burglar, an' other pathrites." Mr.
Hennessy feels sorry for patriots still fervent when their time has
lapsed, but Dooley reminds him that sympathies change with
personal advantage: "It's what Father Kelly calls a case iv
mayhem et chew 'em [*meum et tuum*]. That's Latin, Hinnissy;
an' it manes what's wan man's food is another man's pizen"
(*Hearts*, 8–12).

But the tide of public sentiment cannot be prejudged.
Lieutenant Richmond Pearson Hobson, having accepted Admiral
Sampson's assignment to scuttle the *Merrimac*, actually failed;
he and his crew sank it in the wrong spot, failed to escape to the
rescue craft, and were taken prisoner by Cervera. Yet Hobson
returned from the war a conquering hero, and Mr. Hennessy
protests the gushing sentiment lavished upon him: "Th' idee iv a
hero standin' up befure thousan's iv men with fam'lies an' bein'
assaulted be ondacint females." Such affection, replies Mr.
Dooley, is "th' way th' good Lord has iv makin' us cow'rds
continted with our lot that he niver med a brave man yet that
wasn't half a fool." Dooley, in reciting the events, deplores
Hobson's taking all the credit while the men of his crew remain
nameless: "An' he tuk some other la-ads,—I frget their names,—
they wasn't heroes, annyhow, but was wurrukin' be th' day; an'
he wint in in his undherclothes, so's not to spoil his suit, an' th'
Castiles hurled death an' desthruction on him. An' it niver
touched him no more thin it did anny wan else; an' thin they
riscued him fr'm himsilf. . . . An' he wint on a lecther tour, an'
here he is" (*Hearts*, 216–21).

The gold standard, supported by President McKinley, Dunne
had personified in a cat named Gold Bonds, tended by a
veterinarian named Heinegagubler (possibly Victor George
Heisler) who thereby won an appointment as surgeon-general
and became known as the Stall Angel, "and countless thousands

iv sick hor-rses blessed him" (*Peace*, 77-80). When President McKinley came to Chicago, many heroes contended with him for credit for winning the war. Dooley refused as "prisidint iv this liquor store" to go to hear the speech but read it and about it in the paper: "Th' proceedin's was opened with a prayer that Providence might r-remain undher th' protection iv th' administhration." He continues his version of the speech: " 'Th' nation is wanst more at peace undher th' gran' goold standard,' he says. 'Now,' he says, 'th' question is what shall we do with th' fruits iv victhry?' he says." Dooley's version attains the high sentiment of Henry Cabot Lodge's conclusion to his book on the war, when Lodge foresaw a world divided between the English speaking peoples and the other nations with "the opening of this new epoch and of this mighty conflict" dated from the War of 1898.[17] So Dooley's McKinley concludes, " 'I will tur-rn th' job over to destiny,' he says . . . 'undher an administhration that, thanks to our worthy President an' his cap-ble an' earnest advisers, is second to none,' he says" (*Peace*, 81-86; also see Ellis's *America*, 118-19).

Events of the war, as in the problem of what to do with the Philippines, lingered long after its actual close. Dunne's "Alcohol as Food" essay came out of the army surgeon's announcement that "people shud dhrink in thim hot climates" and that the place should be made more homelike for the Americans stationed there (*Philosophy*, 149-53). The returned hero Admiral Dewey decided to capitalize on his fame by running for president, but Dooley knew that Cousin George knew nothing about politics and said, "Th' reason a sailor thries to ride a horse is because he niver r-rode wan befure" (*Philosophy*, 175-80). To recognize their returning hero's efforts, the public had given Dewey a house but he incurred their wrath by deeding it to his wife, a Catholic. Dunne began his essay "Public Gratitude" with Dooley's demoting the former "Cousin George" to an abrupt "This man Dewey" and reporting the public's new disavowal of him: "Why, he r-run away at th' battle iv Manila." But Dunne left for the conclusion the defense of Dewey's action: "If 'twas a crime f'r an American citizen to have his property in his wife's name they'd be close quarthers in th' pinitinchry" (*Philosophy*, 135-40). Ellis writes, "The admiral, hurt beyond understanding by the outcry he had raised, read the piece and wrote Dunne a stiff letter of thanks" (*America*, 144).

To tell "The Truth about Schley" Dunne again adopted the technique of "Public Gratitude"—having Mr. Dooley voice public opinion in all its fickleness and viciousness, personalizing the events, and supporting the victim. Though Schley had once been credited with the victory at Santiago in Sampson's absence, he was subsequently persecuted, as Long called it, by the press. Dooley begins, "If they'se wan thing I'm prouder iv thin another in me past life . . . 'tis that whin me counthry called me to go to th' Spanish war, I was out. I owe me rayspictibility an' me high standin' among me fellow men to th' fact, Hinnissy, that where th' shot an' shell fell thickest, I wasn't there." Further, he says, "I'd have Congress sthrike medals f'er th' absentee hayroes." Dooley sees the unfortunate publicity generated by the Court of Inquiry as consistent with the fall of other heroes: "First they was Hobson. He kissed a girl an' ivrybody says: 'Hang him. Kill th' coal-scuttler.'" (The last refers to Hobson's subsequent job with Dewey in the Philippines, as Dunne had mentioned in "The Performances of Lieutenant Hobson.") Dooley gives a second example: "Thin they was Dewey. He got marrid an' th' people was f'r makin' mathrimony a penal offince." Maximo Gomez (1826–1905), the "George Wash'n'ton iv th' Ant Hills," had placed his troops at the disposal of the United States Army but in 1899 had been deposed as commander by the Cuban assembly because he had accepted payment from the United States; therefore, in New York, Dooley says, instead of being given the once-promised keys of the city, he was "free to go an' come without annybody payin' anny attintion to him."

"An' now," says Dooley, "it's Schley's turn. . . . Ye used to think he was a gran' man." Now it appears Schley was a coward and an absentee even before he left Tampa: "He was chloryformed an' kep' undher hatches till th' ship was off th' coast iv Floridy. Whin he come to, he fainted at th' sight iv a Spanish ditchnry [dictionary] an' whin a midshipman wint by with a box iv Castile soap, he fell on th' deck writhin' in fear an' exclaimed: 'Th' war is over. I'm shot.'" After a series of inventions showing Schley's eagerness to surrender and another series showing Cervera's courage, Dooley says, " 'Tis a good thing f'r th' United States that me frind Sampson come back at th' r-right moment an' with a few well-directed wurruds to a tillygraft operator, secured th' victhry." The case begins to look worse than it did for Dewey: "So they've arristed Schley. As soon as th' book come out th' Sicrety iv th' Navy issued a warrant again him, chargin' him with victhry an' he's goin' to have to stand thrile f'r it." Only the enemy is safe from public opinion: "Noble ol' Cerveera done nawthin' to disgrace his flag. He los' his ships an' his men an' his biler an' ivrything except his ripytation. He saved that be bein' a good swimmer an' not bein' an officer iv th' United States Navy" (*Opinions*, 101-106).

Just as confusing as the "revisionist" view of individuals, the role of nations also changed, and it soon became apparent that the United States owed its victory to any number of foreign nations: "Some wan power shtretched out its hand [to slap Spain] an' said, 'No. No,' it said, 'thus far but no farther. We will not permit this misguided but warrum-hearted little people [the United States] to be crushed by th' ruffyan power iv Spain,'" Dooley says, though he cannot tell which nation intervened on behalf of the United States (*Observations*, 107-11).

Dunne's Mr. Dooley had never been swayed by the virtues of the white man's burden, and his long dissertation on "The Philippine Peace," speaking for Senator Beveridge, "who was down there f'r tin minyits wanst," shows the Senator with much Dooley humor describing the beauty of that "mos' lovely pearl"; its climate where kissed by the sun makes Dooley think "bitten wud be a betther wurrud"; its politics where "th' office seeks th' man" but unfortunately "it usually happens that those ilicted have not yet surrindhered"; and the islands' produce, of which "All th' riches iv Cathay, all th' wealth iv Ind, as Hogan says, wud look like a second morgedge on an Apache wickeyup compared with th' untold an' almost unmintionable products iv that gloryous domain." Spain had ceded Puerto Rico, the Philippine Islands, and Guam to the United States; and the United States had adopted from Spain its "reconcenthration" as a means of using force against the natives. America's most effective persuasion Dooley knows as "th' wather cure," with which the Filiipino must be "placed upon th' grass an' given a dhrink, a baynit bein' fixed in his mouth so he cannot reject th' hospitality," and then forced down his throat. With the imposition of the American jury system, a Filipino "can be thried but he can't thry his fellow man" (*Observations*, 115-20).

The blessings of liberty accorded to generals who remain heroes earn Mr. Dooley's envy. Generals rise quickly from the ranks of private to positions above examination of their conduct;

a general put on trial inevitably has a friend address the court: "Gintlemen,' says he, 'th' question befure th' coort is not so much did our gallant leader hammer th' coon as wether our flag wanst stuck up where we have wathered so many precious citizens shall iver come down.' (Th' coort: 'No, no!')." Policemen and soldiers are analogous; they are both round-headed. But the life of the policeman is the hard one: "He can't rethreat f'r reinfoorcemints or surrindher with all th' honors iv war. If he surrindhers, he's kilt an' if he rethreats, his buttons comes off" (*Observations*, 123-29).

American imperialism began to pose for Hogan, a prophet ("a man that foresees throuble") the problems of the "rising of the subject races," or "to rejooce us fair wans to their own complexion be batin' us black and blue." Showing Dunne's (hence Dooley's) advancement over the social consciousness of others, represented by Hogan, the essay contains some of Dooley's best satire on American imposition of religion on others, exploration and renaming of others' rivers, construction of "palashal goluf-coorses in the cimitries an' what was wanst th' tomb iv Hung Chang, th' gr-reat Tartar Impror, rose to th' dignity iv bein' th' bunker guardin' th' fifth green," and many more examples follow (*Says*, 50-58).

IV *The War Game Continues*

Everything Dooley criticized about America and its imperialistic forays in "The Rising of the Subject Races" applied just as well to England in South Africa, except that at least one subject, the Dutch, was also white. Of the rivers, Dooley said, "We sint explorers up th' Nile who raypoorted that th' Ganzain flows into th' Oboo just above Lake Mazap, a fact that th' naygurs had known f'r a long time" (*Says*, 56). The Dutch settled in 1652; but England captured the Cape in 1806 and then, without consulting the natives, in 1814 paid 6 million pounds sterling to the Dutch for the country. While the Dutch continued to multiply and the English continued to settle, the English imposed their language and courts on the Dutch and precipitated The Great Trek of about 10,000 Dutch beyond the Orange River in 1836. These became the Boers, whose republic of Natalia the English demolished and whose territory between the Orange and the Vaal Rivers the English later annexed, building a fort in the area. But with troubles elsewhere in Africa, the British, in treaties of 1852 and 1854, released the Dutch to manage themselves as two republics, the Transvaal and the Orange Free State.

The British had another change of heart, however, when it seemed the Dutch government was too weak to protect British interests; and in 1877 they reannexed the country. At this time the people of the Dutch states distrusted their president because of his theological errors (a state of mind which Dooley repeated in references to their fighting with Bibles) but yet opposed the imposition of British government; the two Dutch states joined forces to defeat the British in Natal in 1881, whereupon the British declared them autonomous and in a treaty of 1884 enlarged the Dutch rights in the Transvaal and gave it the name the South African Republic. But sentiment changed in 1885 with the discovery of gold in the Transvaal; and, though of varied nationalities, many of the immigrants coming for gold were British. The Dutch now decided to adopt British tactics: keep the immigrants but exclude them from political power. These immigrants, growing discontented with Dutch politics, came to be called *Uitlanders* and knew the Boers as ignorant and rude people whose culture belonged to the seventeenth century; Dooley pictures them as "us" in being "pursued be th' less fleet but more ignorant Boers peltin' us with guns full iv goold an' bibles." As 1895 began, the immigrants planned to rise against the Dutch government under the presidency of Paul Kruger, whose Transvaal people were now far outnumbered by the Uitlanders but who were well equipped with rifles. A precipitous rising known as the Jameson Raid, in December 1895, ended in defeat of the British and the subsequent union of the two Dutch republics in a treaty promising to defend each other. James Bryce writes that what the English wanted in part was "to bring down the pride of the Dutch, to vindicate the supremacy of England in South Africa"; but the immediate cause of the war was the length of time the immigrants were required to live in the Transvaal before being given the right to vote.[18]

In *Mr. Dooley's Philosophy* Dunne reprinted the six essays on the Boer War, all filled with the same fine attention to detail which characterized the essays on the Spanish-American War. "Well," Dooley says, "th' English heerd they was goold be th' bucket in ivry cellar . . . an' they come on in gr-reat hordes,

sturdy Anglo-Saxons fr'm Saxony, th' Einsteins an' Heidlebacks
an' Werners an' whin they took out goold enough so's they
needed raycreation they wanted to vote." But Kruger says, " 'I'm
not more thin half crazy an' annytime ye find me givin' annywan
a chanst to vote me into a job dhrivin' a mule an' put in an English
prisidint iv this raypublic,' he says, 'ye may conclude that ye'er
Uncle Paul needs a guarjeen!' he says." But finally Dooley claims
that if he had been president there would have been no war:
" 'I'd give thim th' votes,' said Mr. Dooley. 'But,' he added
significantly, 'I'd do th' countin'.' "

"War and War Makers" features various war leaders in several
parts of the world discussing war movements while themselves
removed from the war scenes. Dooley wishes "it cud be fixed up
so's th' men that starts th' wars could do th' fightin'." His essay
"Underestimating the Enemy" tells about his own dream of
emerging victorious in a fight for his rights and sets up the
analogy of the Boers' dream. From June 5, 1900, when the British
occupied Pretoria, the gold mines were in their possession and it
would seem that the war was over; but the Boers continued their
guerrilla warfare for two years, and when the war ended the
British had lost 5,774 killed and 22,829 wounded while the Boers
had lost around 4,000 killed. Dooley accurately summarizes the
differences in warfare: "Th' British marches up with their bands
playin' an' their flags flyin'. An' th' Boers squat behind a
bouldher or a three or set comfortable in th' bed iv a river an'
bang away. Their on'y thradition is that it's betther to be a live
Boer thin a dead hero. . . . They haven't been taught f'r
hundherds iv years that 'tis a miracle f'r to be an officer an' a
disgrace to be a private sojer." But he entertains no doubt that
the British invaded the Dutch, and Dooley concludes, "I'm goin'
to apologize to Shafter. He may not have anny medals f'r standin'
up in range iv th' guns but, be hivins, he niver dhrove his
buckboard into a river occypied be th' formerly loathed Castile."

In that essay, Dooley remarks of newspapers, "I'm a man that's
been through columns an' columns iv war." In the next essay,
"The War Expert," he satirizes war reporters who sit away from
the front with their typewriters and not only construct events as
they might have happened but also presume to direct the
maneuvers; then there is another kind who "gives it good to th'
gover'mint," so that Dooley predicts that it is not the rapid-fire
gun but experts who will make future wars impossible.

"Modern Explosives" discusses new kinds of weapons, especially the chemical explosive lyddite, which turned everything green: "Wanst th' field was r-red, now 'tis a br-right lyddite green. Wanst a man wint out an' died f'r his countrhy, now they sind him out an' lyddite dyes him." The new long-range weapons kept the soldier safe behind the lines and Dooley could well satirize this kind of warfare; but lyddite was named for a town in Britain, and everyone expected Britain to win the war eventually. Dooley admits, "Th' nation that fights with a couplin' pin extinds its bordhers at th' cost iv th' nation that fights with a clothes pole."

The United States kept itself neutral, though it would appear that any country fighting for its independence (especially from Britain, as the United States did) would find here much sympathy and aid. But in the face of British triumph, Dooley said, "Th' amount of sympathy that goes out f'r a shrugglin' people is reg'lated, Hinnissy, be th' amount iv shrugglin' th' people can do. Th' wurruld, me la-ad, is with th' undher dog on'y as long as he has a good hold an' a chanst to tur-rn over." In "The Boer Mission," Dooley shows several American leaders hiding from the emissaries: William Jennings Bryan; Secretary Hay, who says he "sint me own son into ye'er accursed but liberty-lovin' counthry"; and even President Mack, who extends his sympathy unofficially, for "Me official hear-rt,' he says, 'is not permitted be th' constitootion to throb durin' wurrukin' hours,' he says." (The above essays are from *Philosophy*, 35–75.)

Into the terms of the Peace of Vereeniging the British wrote certain facts of the war: the destruction of farm properties and the repatriation of burghers who declared themselves subjects of King Edward II. In "Disqualifying the Enemy," Dooley said, "How th' Boers sthud up to it, Hinissy, I niver can tell. I've been countin' up their casulties, an' they've lost enough cows to keep Armour goin' a year." Earlier, by the close of 1899, the British had needed more soldiers and called upon citizens as volunteers; for this reason Dooley presents the British side in the peace negotiations: " 'We can't keep three hundhred thousan' sojers an' th' rapid-fire pote Roodyard Kipling down there f'river. We need th' warryors at home to dhrive th' busses an' lade th' cotillyons an' they hasn't been a good pome on th' butther an' egg market, th' price iv stocks, th' prospects iv th' steel thrade, th' opening iv th' new undherground or th' mannyfacther iv bicycles since Roodyard wint away." The terms of the peace agreement indicated that the war ended when the British said it did, and on their terms, so that Dooley calls them "a sporrtin' people" and explains the title of this essay: "They'll race anny man's horse in th' wurruld if th' jockey won't sit th' way he thinks will make th' horse go fast. They'll row anny crew in th' wurruld if th' crew will train on beer an' cigareets an' won't be in a hurry to get through. An' whin it comes to war, they have th' r-rest iv creation sittin' far back in th' rear iv th' hall. We have to lick our inimny. They disqualify him" (*Opinions*, 29–34).

In October 1900 Kruger returned to Europe, and on October 25 the Transvaal was ceremoniously annexed. But more than a year later, on Christmas Eve, De Wet captured a large number of the British yeomanry, and in the spring commander Paul Methuen of the British was taken prisoner by De La Rey. Dooley attributes this last event to the British decision to stop fighting. His essay "The End of the War" satirizes the British arrangement of supplies, including pianos and pianolas and such in the deployment, but then "Th' great heart [of the British nation] begun to grumble, which is a way th' great heart iv a nation has. It ast what was th' use iv this costly manoover—if they was as manny gin'rals left afther it as befure" (*Observations*, 191–95). From Mr. Dooley's viewpoint, everything happens, for whatever perverse reason, and falls into a rational scheme.

The "hands across the sea"—Dooley's method of referring to international connections—now stretched to form an alliance between Great Britain and Japan (1902) which strengthened Japan's hopes of driving the Russians out of Manchuria. The Russo-Japanese War (1904–1905), fought in China, set Dooley thinking once more that, without reference to the Boxer rebellion, a boxing match would be a good analogy for the way wars should be fought—with kings and emperors fighting each other in person. "War wud be wan continyous manoover," he said in "War," with "wan iv thim manooverin' west an' th' other manooverin' east. They'd niver meet till years afther th' gloryous sthruggle" (*Dissertations*, 207–10). In "Sieges," Hennessy sympathizes with the starving lads in besieged Port Arthur but Dooley recalls the earlier retreat of the British diplomats into the Embassy in Peking (1900) as a time of looting; now he decides to save his tears until the stock market and other reports come in. Here is an older Dooley wearying of war and its repetitions, saying, "It's always th' same way. Wan iv th' sthrangest things about life is that it will go on in onfav'rable circumstances an' go out whin ivrything is aisy." People become accustomed to bombardment and go on living, but, Dooley says, "I bet ye no garrison iver rayfused to surrindher whin it was starv-in', onless it was afraid th' inimy wud shoot th' man with th' white flag" (*Dissertations*, 285–90).

United States sympathies had been with Japan, and Dooley recalls in "A Broken Friendship" a time when Hogan sang "Gawd Save th' Mickydoo" with a Japanese friend. Now, however, Dooley asks, "D'ye raymimber how we hollered with joy whin a Rooshyan Admiral put his foot through th' bottom iv a man-iv-war an' sunk it." But after Roosevelt had been awarded the Nobel Peace Prize for his efforts in settling the war, the United States failed to back Japanese claims for indemnity from Russia, and the Japanese failed to keep the "gentlemen's agreement" which would have controlled the flow of immigrants into the United States, so that Dooley expresses altered American feelings: "They were th' gr-reatest liars in th' wurruld an' formerly friends iv th' Prisidint." A corresponding expression of the Japanese feeling comes in a note to the President: "Oh, brother beloved, we adore ye. Had ye not butted in with ye'er hively binivolence we wud've shook Rooshya down f'r much iv her hateful money." But possession of the Philippines had made the United States irrevocably an Asian power, and Dooley concludes with hoping that we could have signed a treaty of peace with Japan "an' with tears iv humilyation in our eyes handed thim th' Philippeens!" (*Says*, 100–109).

In "The Japanese Scare," Dooley dealt with the altered personal relationships attendant upon the fears that war with Japan was imminent, with people being careful how they spoke of a Japanese, and "Tiddy Rosenfelt is discovered undher a bed with a small language book thryin' to larn to say 'Spare me' in th' Jap'nese tongue." Dooley laments times passed—"In th' good old days we wudden't have thought life was worth livin' if we cudden't insult a foreigner"—and part of the sensitivity stems from different lifestyles and ethics, including the kamikaze: "Most sojers don't like to be kilt. A Jap'nese sojer prefers it." Finally Dooley decides "There ar-re no frinds at cards or wurruld pollyticks. Th' deal changes an' what started as a frindly game iv rob ye'er neighbor winds up with an old ally catchin' me pullin' an ace out iv me boot an' denouncin' me" (*Says*, 193-203).

But war could be regarded as a game, as Dooley determined in "The War Game," if the new international consciousness of the United States deemed it worthy of enemy attack. So the army and navy set up a "thrile iv cunnin' an' darin'" by means of which "we larn whether th' inimy cud sneak into Boston after dark without annywan seein' thim an' anchor in Boston common." Dooley decides, after close description of the maneuvers, that the loser is the treasury (*Observations*, 231-36).

The failure of the second Hague Conference (1907) produced Dunne's usual superb satire, as he reduced its proposals to the level of affairs actually settled: "Th' Hon'rable Joe Choate moved that in future wars no miliatry band shud be considered complete without a base-dhrum. Carrid. . . . Th' Hon'rable Joe Choate moved that in all future wars horses shud be fed with hay whereiver possible. Carrid." Finally the meeting devolved into a discussion of what war is, and the delegate from China gives a frightening example only to be told it was only an expedition, not a war, "'to serve th' high moral jooties iv Christyan civvyliza- tion.' 'Thin,' says th' dillygate fr'm Chiny, puttin' on his hat, 'I'm f'r war,' he says. 'It ain't so rough,' he says. An' he wint home" (*Says*, 204-13).

The major wars had kept Dunne continually engaged with the topic — the Spanish-American (1898), the Boer War (1899-1902), the Russo-Japanese (1904-1905) — for roughly fifty essays. Dunne had written also on the Civil War, a commemora- tive piece for the second book entitled "The Blue and the Gray" for Memorial Day which features a person not having been in the war opposed to a war monument, and another called "On Food in War" for his last book. In addition, war and warlike discussions appeared in numerous other essays, so that it naturally follows that Dunne should have been depressed by World War I (1914-1918) and generally refuse to write about it.

In "On Past Glories" Dooley recalls his participation in the glories of war through reading about them, particularly in such works as Charles Lever's *Charles O'Malley* (1841), a gay and whimsical picture of an Irish dragoon in the Napoleonic Wars. Now, however, Dooley objects that "what with their gases an' their bombs war's no longer a career f'r a gintleman. . . . Why, they ain't aven a declaration iv war in these days, or if there is wan, it's put out a month or two afther th' war begins durin' a lull in th' fightin'.'" He says, "There are lots iv things in th' back iv th' dhrug store they haven't thried so far." And, waxing prophetic, he does not believe "there'll iver be peace in this fractious wurruld. But th' time may come whin war as it is to-day will be abolished" (*Will*, 198–211).

The Prohibition movement forced itself into the war effort, and Dunne wrote "The Army Canteen" with Mr. Dooley protesting that his own objections to the army's serving beer went to naught; but when the Young Ladies' Christian Temperance Union marched their complaint to Congress, the canteen was abolished. He knows that Mars, the god of war, "was no good onless he was pushed into throuble be Backis, the gawd iv dhrink"; and he sees drink as important for making a man think he's better: "A little iv it lifts ye out iv th' mud where chance has thrown ye; a little more makes ye think th' stains on ye'er coat ar-re eppylets; a little more dhrops ye back into th' mud again." Dooley would not have chosen to be a bartender except that he was "too selfish to be a mechanic an' too tender-hearted to be a banker or a lawyer." But the women should remember that drink "has caused manny a lady to be loved that otherwise might've died single" (*Says*, 110–22).

In 1926 Mr. Dooley spoke his last word on war, but did it by satirizing the stay-at-home patriots who were busy finding reasons not to enlist, being chased by war-bond salespeople, saluting the majors and the colonels, learning that "Keep the Home Fires Burning" meant the price of coal was going up, and spying on possible spies. Schwartzmeister arouses suspicion with a series of three lights in his house. He explains, "I was me pipe lightin'. It's these verdamft matches," and gets himself arrested for insulting one of our great industries. When Hennessy asks if Dooley thinks we'll ever have another war, Dooley replies, "Not ontil this wan is over. It'll take us th' rest iv our lives to get it out iv our system" (*Liberty*, February 27, 1926, 45–48).

CHAPTER 5

When "Peace Wanst More Wags Her Wings over th' Counthry"

"THEY can't hurt us with their lies. We have th' guns an' we'll bate thim yet." Hennessy with these words, in "Minister Wu" on the Chinese situation, adapts to the problems of lasting peace the "famous last words" of Kruger as he faced the English at the outbreak of the Boer War (*Philosophy*, 83–89). In "War Recollections," Dooley said, "Now peace broods over Europe to such an extint that th' population can't see their way to pay their debts" (*Liberty*, May 8, 1926). One of his frequent topics, sports, proves a natural alternative to war, as football moves out of the oats field of his youth and into the public arena with sufficient equipment for both attack and defense laden on one human body: "I seen th' Dorgan la-ad comin' up th' sthreet yesterday in his futball clothes,—a pair iv matthresses on his legs, a pillow behind, a mask over his nose, an' a bushel measure iv hair on his head" (*Peace*, 152–57). Athletics, Dooley determined, came from the English, who "have a sayin' over there that th' jook iv Wellinton said first or somebody said fr him an' that's been said a number iv times since, that th' battle iv Watherloo was won on th' playin' fields iv Eton." Athletics change the home life drastically, for women who can swing a golf club do not resort to weeping; and Dooley admits, "I'm afraid I cud not love a woman I might lose a fight to" (*Opinions*, 79–84).

Dunne, in his first essay for *Liberty* magazine, rose to the defense of football player Red Grange, who in 1924 made four touchdowns in fifteen minutes; the trouble began when the hero tried to find a job teaching languages. This essay contains fine satire on universities and their use of football, among which Dooley observes that "Jawn D. give no money to th' colledges befure futball was inthrajooced (*Liberty*, February 13, 1926).

The peaceful activities of Americans, sometimes inseparable from their wartime activities, provided Dunne a range of topics—pastimes and holidays, international politics and problems, national issues, characters, and criminals.

I Pastimes and Holidays

Dooley perceives a distinct difference between golf and football, for the score in golf is computed by social standing. For example, "If ye bring ye'er wife f'r to see th' game, an' she has her name in the paper, that counts ye wan" (*Peace*, 249-54). Since his own social standing enabled him to play with presidents, Dunne in later years could answer from personal experience when Hennessy asks Dooley, "Is th' President a good goluf player, d'ye know, at all?" Dooley replies, "As a goluf player he cud give Lincoln a sthroke a hole." But he begins the discussion by describing golf players who do not work at it—such as Hogan, who slaves at it. The perversities of the game turn the best of friends into enemies: "All I can say about it is that it's a kind iv a game iv ball that ye play with ye'er own worst inimy which is ye-ersilf, an' a man ye don't like goes around with ye an' gloats over ye, an' a little boy follows ye to carry th' clubs an' hide th' ball afther ye've hit it" (*Will*, 144-58).

That the sturdy English could occasionally win an event Mr. Dooley and history both had to admit. Always, however, their parentage of this upstart and relatively uncivilized land proved a reprimand to American enthusiasm. Attending the Olympic games, Dooley says, "They was an Englishman standin' behind me, Hinnissy, an' he was a model iv behavior f'r all Americans intindin' to take up their homes in Cubia. Ye cudden't get this la-ad war-rmed up if ye built a fire undher him." Dunne makes adequate use of the connection between Cambridge University of England and Harvard of Cambridge, Massachusetts, and of the Americanization of a Bodley, subtly omitting reference to Cambridge University's ancient enemy in sports, Oxford, and the famed Bodleian library at Oxford University: " 'If all th' la-ads enthered into th' r-races with th' same spirit ye show now,' I says, 'th' English flag'd be dhroopin' fr'm th' staff, an' Cyrus Bodley in Wadham, Mass., 'd be paintin' th' stars an' stripes on th' Nelson monnymint' [symbol of English domination in Dublin, Ireland], I says." For American observers of the Olympic games, Dooley

says, "Ye get to th' Olympian games be suffocation in a tunnel.
Whin ye come to, ye pay four shillin's or a dollar in our degraded
currency, an' stand in th' sun an' look at th' Prince iv Wales. Th'
Prince iv Wales looks at ye, too, but he don't see ye" (*Philosophy*,
201–207).

An international incident that developed from the America's
Cup yachting race pitted the American Jack Larsen against Irish-
born Sir Thomas Johnstone Lipton, whose five yachts, each
named *Shamrock*, were defeated in 1899, 1901, 1903, 1920, and
1930. Regulations enacted after a Lipton defeat determined not
only the size of the vessels but also the color of the wallpaper,
according to Mr. Dooley, who maintained that a yacht club "is an
assocyation, Hinnissy, iv mimbers iv th' Bar." A yacht race
consists of " 'Lave us go an' see our lawyers.' 'Tis 'Haul away on
th' writ iv ne exeat,' an' 'Let go th' peak capias.' 'Tis 'Pipe all
hands to th' Supreme Coort.' 'Tis 'A life on th' boundin' docket
an' a home on th' rowlin' calendar' " (*Opinions*, 71–75). As for
international affairs, he found that England was losing her
supremacy because "Englishmen get down to their jobs at iliven
o'clock figurin' a goluf scoor on their cuffs an' lave at a quarther
to twelve on a bicycle" (*Opinions*, 79–84). But difficulties in
Venezuela, Alaska, and Canada seemed trivial beside the
importance of sports: "some day we'll be beat in a yacht r-race or
done up at futball an' thin what Hogan calls th' dogs iv war'll
break out iv th' kennel an' divastate th' wurruld" (*Philosophy*,
201).

But Mr. Dooley gives up on "the higher baseball," for which he
now admits not having the intellect; it distinctly contrasts with
the baseball of his youth and now requires "an absolute masthry
iv th' theery iv ballistic motion." In his youth, he says, "No man
was very good at it that was good at annything else," and there is
a pronounced discrepancy now between the report of analysts
and the comment of a player. According to the analysts, "Th'
purpose iv th' batsman is, afther judgin' be scientific methods th'
probable coorse or thrajecthry iv th' missile to oppose it with
sufficyent foorce at th' proper moment an' at th' most efficient
point, first to retard its forward movement, thin to correct th'
osseylations an' fin'ly to propel it in a direction approximately
opposite fr'm its original progress." Mr. Dooley's noble intention
to spend an afternoon at the chemical laboratory for his baseball
edification suffers rude alteration of purpose when he interviews

Petie Donahue, who became a famous hitter after being dismissed from the Christian Brothers school because he could not add. Petie would like access to that scientific information to even out the valleys in his record, "to find out how I do it whin I do it an' why I don't do it whin I don't," he says. Asked when he pitches best, he says, "A day or two befure I sign me conthract" (*Will*, 92–101).

Mr. Dooley had long maintained that the best activity would be inactivity, that wealth should secure exactly that, in opposition to the careers of the wealthy who proved they were wealthy by killing themselves with sporting work. "At a Summer Resort" shows people trying to be happy out of town; Dooley returns to Chicago (*Will*, 27–42).

The reverses of fortune which turn work into sport and vice versa Dooley finds in the history of his friend Higgins, who formerly hated driving horses for a brewery but, now that he has wealth, must exercise a horse "to keep th' horse in good health"; who formerly despised Swede sailors, now has to sail a yacht; now has to run an automobile, "which is th' same thing as dhrivin' a throlley car on a windy day without pay; he has to play golf, which is th' same thing as bein' a letther-carryer without a dacint unifrom; he has to play tennis, which is another wurrud f'r batin' a carpet . . . he has to go abroad, which is th' same thing as bein' an immigrant . . . an' he has to play cards with a man that knows how, which is th' same thing as bein' a sucker." Dooley summarizes all this with the remark that "a rich man at spoort is a kind iv non-union laborer," and "th' poor ar-re th' on'y people that know how to injye wealth." This, he decides, must be because the one great object in every man's life is to get tired enough to sleep: "Wurruk is wurruk if ye'er paid to do it an' it's a pleasure if ye pay to be allowed to do it" (*Observations*, 175–79). Writing on the "Pleasures of the Rich" vacationing in Florida and altering the landscape, Dooley says, "As th' pote says, th' proper study iv mankind is man, an' if it's improper it's aven more inthrestin'" (*Liberty*, March 20, 1926). In "The Effects of Spring" he comments on people engaged in catching colds and falling in love that "I'm told we live in a timp'rate climate. If so, I wisht it wud take to dhrink f'r a change" (*Liberty*, April 24, 1926).

The British return in the form of a manager of a gambling establishment. When Mr. Dooley interviews him, he naively but

forthrightly announces that "In ivry other business in life th'
ilimint iv chance enthers in. But not in mine." He complains of
the dull, monotonous grind broken only by incidents such as that
last week when "wan iv me op-ratives sprained his wrist . . .
takin' th' money fr'm an expert accountant, who had a system
that no wan cud bate." Mr. Dooley takes him by the hand and
asks sympathetically, "Is there no way iv increasin' th' chances
again' ye?" to give him the boon of some diversion. He replies,
"None . . . while there ar-re so manny people with pear-shaped
heads" (*Dissertations,* 153–58). In "The Skirts of Chance," Mr.
Dooley tells how to manage a nickel-in-the-slot machine
philosophically for profit (*Hearts,* 56–60), and in "The Church
Fair" how to keep the money from a winner (*Hearts,* 135–38).

The Game of Cards, complicated subject that it is, requires
elaborate analysis by Dooley of both victim and operator.
Reporting a speech by a professional gambler at a gambling
convention, Dooley says, "Th' war has made frightful inroads on
their customers, manny iv whom have gone to th' front an' got
what was comin' to thim. He was glad to be able to say that so far
as he knew not a single pro-fissyonal gambler had enlisted in this
horrible and needless sthrife." Gambling itself he finds a
variation of the ancient shell game, except in this game the shells
were loaded. International card sharks found they must focus on
America, "land iv opportunity, where a wise guy is born ivery
half minyit." Hogan's addiction to gambling plays out its luckless
fate, with Dooley's usual success at presenting two sides of any
one subject: the professional has "a weary, pained look," but in
Hogan's eyes there is "a bright light iv hopeless but happy
avarice" (*Will,* 159–74).

Holidays as national milestones mark the resolution of the
individual and the progress of the American dream. Christmas
predictably provides Dooley an opportunity to explain the
supreme outlandishness of gifts he received and the deafness of
friends who cannot take hints about the one small item he does
want (*Peace,* 223–28). New Year's helps him to realize how
important his enemies are for helping him to define himself, and
he and Dorsey resolve to continue their unjustly founded enmity
(*Peace,* 95–99).

"Keeping Lent" shows Father Kelly at his most humane: he
assures Dooley that "Starvation don't always mean salvation,"
and has half a lump of sugar in his hot toddy (*Hearts,* 185–89). In

later years Dooley decides the model of the saints is outmoded
because, as his Uncle Mike of the previous generation protested,
"Th' Lives iv th' Saints f'r eighteen hundred an' fifty ain't out
yet." Besides, the most effective virtues result from plain
common sense. Dooley says, "I'm tim'prate because too much
dhrink doesn't agr-ree with me; modest because I look best that
way; gin'rous because I don't want to be thought stingy; honest
because iv th' polis force; an' brave whin I can't r-run away"
(*Dissertations,* 123–26). Mr. Dooley sees the Thanksgiving
turkey, amid many national divergences, the "common barnyard
fowl" that hitches the nation together in one mutual celebration.
Father Kelly, however, says the holiday was founded by the
Puritans to give thanks for being preserved from the Indians and
that "we keep it to give thanks we are presarved fr'm th'
Puritans." It was they who taught the Indians religion and
slavery, and now the day seems most faithfully violated when
"th' churches is open an' empty, the fleet anise seed bag is
pursooed over th' smilin' potato patch an' th' groans iv th' dyin'
resound fr'm manny a futball field" (*Opinions,* 125–29).

Reading books as a pastime presents the old problems of
choosing quality literature. Rudyard Kipling, for example,
Dooley says sleeps "with his poetic pants in his boots beside his
bed" like a fireman, and leaps into poetry at the slightest
provocation: "He's prisident iv th' Pome Supply Company,—fr-
resh pothry delivered ivry day at ye'er dure (*Hearts,* 13–17). Mr.
Dooley knows that his opinion of Kipling differs from that of the
general public (Kipling received the Nobel prize for literature in
1907), but he based part of Kipling's popularity on his illness in
the United States, when "th' sicker he got, th' bigger man he was.
Ivry time his timprachoor wint up, his repytation as a pote
advanced tin degrees." The popularity waned when he
recovered, however, and Mr. Dooley reports reading a scholarly
article in the paper, calling Kipling a "confidence o'rator," and
adding "if there is a pressman in this buildin' that cudden't write
a betther wan, we'd feed him to his own press" (*Opinions,*
63–68).

In similar vein, for Hennessy's unsmiling edification, Mr.
Dooley constructs his own Sherlock Holmes case, carefully
explaining how simple it is for a great sleuth. "Simple," says Mr.
Hennessy, "'tis foolish." When Dooley unravels the disap-
pearance of a dog, Hennessy reminds him the dog has been

returned, whereupon Dooley complains that with Sherlock Holmes "Nawthin' happens in rale life that's complicated enough f'r him!" Crime, he says, is "a pursoot iv th' simple-minded. Th' other kind, th' uncatchable kind that is took up be men iv intellict is called high fi-nance" (*Observations*, 23–29).

Theodore Roosevelt popularized a book called *The Simple Life* (1901) by French author Charles Wagner, saying that the book contained "such wholesome sound doctrine that I wish it could be used as a tract throughout our country." Clearly, like the poor man's work which becomes rich man's sport, the simple life could be enjoyed only by those who lived without it. The image of a Frenchman being conducted among the wealthy of this country and shown all the technical advances and calling those simple provokes Mr. Dooley to extend the idea: "A poor man walkin' th' sthreet is far less simple [struggling to make a living] thin a rich man lollin' back in his carriage an' figurin' out simple inthrest on his cuff" (*Dissertations*, 229–34).

In "The Food We Eat," Dunne reviews Upton Sinclair's *The Jungle* (1906), an exposé of the Chicago stockyards. Because of it, Dooley can find no suitable food; the novel exaggerates conditions so alarmingly that Dooley reports "Congress decided to abolish all th' days iv th' week except Friday." Hogan writes his own sample novel in *The Jungle* style (*Dissertations*, 247–54).

For the simple man, music fares little better than books. "Slavin contra Wagner" sets up a dramatic confrontation between McKenna's friend Slavin and Molly Donahue's mother, who scorns her daughter's playing anything but Wagner and "Choochooski." When Molly explains that Wagner is the music of the future, Slavin replies, "Yes, but I don't want me hell on earth" (*Hearts*, 125–29). Likewise in "The Serenade" the unsuccessful playing of a cornet attracts a crowd for McKenna's friend Felix Pindergasht but fails to win the heart of Molly Donahue (*Hearts*, 206–209). A night at the Grand Opera permits Dooley to observe some of the people "settin' in seats an' some iv thim in bur-rd cages up above, an' more standin'," and to wonder why some one did not inform the women that "their dhresses was slippin' down"; but the singer "whalin' away in Eyetallian" provides an opportunity for the men to discuss politics and therefore proves very profitable (*Hearts*, 130–34).

Dooley saw the Paris Exposition as a vast scheme to rip off wealthy Americans, who would have to go begging door-to-door

on their return (*Philosophy*, 161-67). Even so, it remained a
status symbol, with many ordinary Americans carefully explaining why they were not going. Dunne's essay on Art Patronage
satirizes the means by which wealthy men become art collectors,
factory-produced reproductions are paraded as rare art, and the
young neighborhood artist becomes an open forger (*Observations*, 41-46).

The play *Cyrano de Bergerac* provides Dooley an opportunity
to improvise not only the famous duel poem about the nose but
also the obviousness of dramatic irony. Hogan as Cyrano at the
end announces one thing has made his life worth living; everyone
in the audience knows it's his nose, but no one on the stage can
guess that. Hogan, however, says, "'Tis me hat,' an', makin' a low
bow to th' audjience, he fell to th' flure so hard that his nose fell
off an' rowled down on Mike Finnegan" (*Hearts*, 228-33).
Dooley reviewed also Edmond Rostand's *L'Aiglon*, by the same
author as the play "about the man with th' big nose, that wud
dhraw a soord or a pome on e'er a man alive." Having known
some evil Napoleons, Mr. Dooley distrusts this son of Napoleon
but relates the events of his life with a "hackin' cough all through
the piece" (*Philosophy*, 103-108). In "The American Stage,"
Dooley admits that Hogan says he does not have the dramatic
delusion, which means "ye can't make me believe that twenty
years has elapsed whin I know that I've on'y had time to pass th'
time iv day with th' bartinder nex' dure." The problems of
creating illusion remain serious: "If day iver broke on th' level th'
way it does on th' stage 'twud tear th' bastin' threads out iv what
Hogan calls th' firmymint" (*Philosophy*, 223-28).

Dooley necessarily took up the problems of vacation and
travel. "The City as a Summer Resort" contains a humorous
account of his fighting mosquitoes on Hogan's farm; and Dooley
returns to the city after only one night of wakefulness with farm
noises, having decided that, contrary to living where produce
comes from, "th' place to live in is where all th' good things iv life
goes to. Ivrything that's worth havin' goes to th' city; th'
counthry takes what's left" (*Opinions*, 45-51). Dunne's essay on
the automobile poses Algernon as millionaire against the poor
people who exaggerate his speed and recklessness and bring
charges against him which land him in jail; instead of strewing
roses for Algernon, the children strew tacks. When Dooley tries
to ride in the automobile, it has a convulsion, and Dooley says

"Something is wr-rong with ye'er ir-n hourse. He's et something that don't agree with him" (*Dissertations,* 67–73). "The Comforts of Travel," one of the most humorous pieces, shows Dooley attempting to sleep on a Pullman bound for Saint Louis, his exit from the top berth as funny as his entrance: "with th' assistance iv th' step-laddher, th' bell-rope, an' th' bald head iv th' man in th' lower berth, I bounded lightly out iv me little nook an' rose fr'm th' flure with no injury worse thin a sprained ankle." All this experience teaches him a definition of comfort: "Comfort is in havin' things where ye can reach thim" (*Dissertations,* 77–83).

In his essay on "Vacations," Dunne returned to the topic of travel by train, dwelling on its many miseries; for example, "A thrain that is goin' to anny iv th' penal colonies where most men spind their vacations will stop at more places thin a boy on an errand. Whiniver it sees a human habitation it will pause an' exchange a few wurruds iv pleasant greetin'. It will stop at annything. It wud stop at nawthin'" (*Says,* 227–39).

Many of the poor Irish leaving their homes during the famine years traveled in what they called "coffin ships," conditions were so crowded and food so scarce. Dooley tells in "The Wanderers" his own experiences of watching a baby die on his crossing to this country (*Hearts,* 139–42), a scene far removed from the luxuries of the later "Ocean Travel." Here he finds ingenious ways to suffer sea sickness without admitting to sea sickness, to give tips to people who disdain taking them, and to defeat the report of his social life on board when it reaches the newspapers before he arrives in port (*Says,* 67–77).

The original sin among status seekers was being born in this country, and William Waldorf Astor "thried to live down to it" by living in London. In "Americans Abroad," Dooley maintains that the Waldorf Astoria had been built for "jooks who had no sins but thim iv their own makin'." In "A Society Scandal" he delights in recounting the incident at a party in Astor's London home when Astor ejected the uninvited Sir William Mills and the ensuing quarrel involved the Prince of Wales (*Philosophy,* 189–93). Dunne had written an early essay "On the Power of Love" about the defeat of boxer James J. Corbett in March 1897, when he lost the title to Robert Fitzsimmons. (Dooley admires Fitzsimmons's wife, of whom he says, "I'd like to have such a wife as that. I'd do th' cookin', an' lave th' fightin' to her.") Now, in "Hotels and Hotel Life," boxing and high society come together, and Dooley delivers one of his profoundest criticisms of the American way. The boxer Jack O'Brien, having been received with enthusiasm in his native city, a celebrity after his 1905 defeat of Robert Fitzsimmons, made the mistake of registering in the Waldorf Astoria. Upon protests from the members of high society, misbehaving in their own way but refusing to stay with a commoner such as O'Brien present, the hotel ejected him. Hennessy says that he heard O'Brien once threw a fight. Keeping in mind the often shady means by which millionaires acquire their wealth and the privilege to misbehave, Dooley replies, "I don't believe it; if he had he wud've been a welcome guest" (*Dissertations*, 237–43).

Dunne's Mr. Dooley believes the wealthy have exploited their fellow man and have used dishonest means for grasping wealth. He numbers among them the railroad magnate George Pullman, whose affairs, brought home to Chicagoans, brought also federal troops under General Miles in 1894 to break a strike; two strikers were killed and several wounded. (Charles Fanning reproduces the Pullman essays in *Mr. Dooley and the Chicago Irish.*) In "The Pursuit of Riches," Dooley compares life to a Pullman dining car, "a fine bill iv fare but nawthin' to eat." He and Hennessy are not rich because they refuse to "cash in" friends, relatives, health, and other forms of happiness (*Dissertations*, 35–39).

II   The Dreyfus Case

Many Americans, not only the patrons of the Waldorf Astoria, had a keen interest in international affairs; and Dunne wrote in all six essays on the confusing issue of France's Dreyfus case. The first, entitled "On the Dreyfus Case" (1898), features Hennessy as anti-Dreyfusard, saying with convincing solemnity, "I don't know anything about it, but I think he's guilty. He's a Jew." Dooley assures Hennessy, "Like most iv ye'er fellow-citizens, ye start impartial. Ye don't know annything about th' case. If ye knew annything, ye'd not have an opinyon wan way or th' other" (*Peace*, 234–38).

Suspected of selling French military secrets to Germany, Dreyfus was convicted of treason by a closed court-martial on December 22, 1894, and was sent to Devil's Island. Two years later, for his suspicions and investigations of Major Walsin-Esterhazy (Dooley's "Estherhazy"), Major Georges Picquart

(Dooley's "Peekhart") was sent to North Africa. At this time Lieutenant Colonel Joseph Henry (Dooley's "Hinnery") took his counterespionage job seriously enough to forge evidence against Dreyfus, for which Dooley calls him "that Col. Hinnery, th' man that sint me frind Cap. Dhry-fuss to th' cage," with the latter a reference to the confinement of Dreyfus on Devil's Island "in hut, double staple [double irons] at night [in] perimeter court round hut with solid palisading, with sentinel inside,"[1] by order of the Minister of the Colonies. Picquart, persisting, was dismissed from the army for "professional faults" but continued his efforts as a private citizen to exonerate Dreyfus. The writer Emile Zola was tried and found guilty of libel. Picquart was arrested for revealing confidential military documents. When the Minister of War, Jacques Cavaignac, admitted the possibility of forgery in the evidence on August 31, 1898, Colonel Henry committed suicide and Esterhazy fled the country.

Dooley's reconstruction of events features a brilliant portmanteau word (*jackass* and *J'accuse*) and a whimsically garbled crime reflecting the contradictions in the case. Admitting that the first trial was secret, he recites a charge against Dreyfus that begins with "the remains of the poor girl" and goes through a series of offhand references to "th' safe afther 'twas blown open," Dreyfus naked in the Devil's Island cage, a shooting, a fire, forging of a will, and stealing of a dog. Zola's "J'Accuse" letter appeared in *L'Aurore* January 13, 1898; and Dooley now pictures Zola interrupting the trial repeatedly, shouting, " 'Jackuse,' which is a hell of a mane thing to say to anny man. An' they thrun him out." Thereafter Zola shouts, "Jackuse" from the doorway, each time being "thrun out." As the trial begins, before testimony, the court decides to send Dreyfus to "th' Divvle's own island," and the defense and the court determine to defend the honor of France by a duel in the street—a reference to actual duels fought between Clemenceau and Drumont on February 28, 1898, and between Picquart and Henry on March 5, 1898. The first investigation of Dreyfus, October 14 to October 31, 1894, was conducted by Lieutenant Colonel du Paty de Clam, whom Dooley names "Pat th' Clam"; and Dooley combines the duels with the suicide of Henry in having Pat th' Clam say, "Th' coort will now adjourn f'r dools, an' all ladin' officers iv th' ar-rmy not in disgrace already will assimble in jail, an' com-mit suicide."

The bewildered Hennessy demands to know what Dreyfus is

charged with, and Dooley replies, "I'll niver tell ye; it's too much to ask. . . . Well, annyhow, he's guilty, ye can bet on that" (*Peace,* 234-38). The Anti-Dreyfusards, as indicated by suicides of French officers and duels among officials, viewed attempts at defense of Dreyfus as efforts to discredit the French army; and the way the French public took up the case and permitted it to divide the nation inspired Dunne's "On the French Character," an essay showing how the English prosper from surrounding territories by persuading the natives that the English desires are right and proper, while the French shouting "À base" dispute their motives among themselves (*Peace,* 255-60).

Although Dunne had a press pass to the retrial of Dreyfus in Rennes, France, from August 7 to September 11, 1899, he remained in England and wrote his scintillating essays, a series of five, as he usually did—reflecting popular opinion as derived from the newspapers. The public ceremony dismissing Captain Dreyfus from the French army, early in January 1895, had been called a degradation, a word which Dooley repeats as a motif in the first of the essays on this second trial. He begins with describing the "little city iv Rennes," now "thronged with des'prit journalists," an opportunity unequaled since the war in Cuba now presenting itself for "these brave fellows gathered together at th' risk iv their lives fr'm overcrowdin' th' resthrants." It is good for France "that there ar-re silf-sacrificin' men that don't undherstand her language, to presint her vicious nature to th' English an' the American public." The French themselves are "disgeezed behind a varnish iv ojoous politeness which our waiters know nawthin' about." Dooley describes for Hennessy the parade outside the courtroom, the appearance of the prisoner, and the scene inside. He records the division of the French nation and the conflicting reports of journalists through opposing descriptions of Dreyfus as he enters the courtroom: "Captain Dhryfuss plainly shows his throubles, which have made him look tin years younger. His raven hair is intirely white; an' his stalwart frame, with th' shoulders thrown back, is stooped and weary. His haggard face was flushed with insolent confidence, an' th' cowa'ridice in his face showed in his fearless eye. As he passed, a young Fr-rinch sojer was with diff'culty resthrained fr'm sthrikin' him an' embracin' him with tears in his eyes."

On August 12 General Auguste Mercier, former war minister,

testified for almost four hours against Dreyfus; finally accuser and accused confronted each other as Dreyfus interrupted. Dooley begins "Gin'ral Merceer's" testimony in the first essay and continues it in the second. One of the most famous secret documents introduced at the trial became known as the "Canaille de D. . . ." The "scoundrel D" thus referred to for stealing fortification plans was a M. Dubois whom the prosecution took to be Dreyfus. The public's familiarity with this term enabled Dunne to have a correspondent in court put a question to "this canal iv a Jew." As Dooley tells about it, the prosecution and its witnesses at every word attempt to defend their actions for the honor of France or some part of it; yet the trial itself in fact reflected that there was little honor anywhere. President Loubet was assaulted by an anti-Dreyfusard on June 4, 1899, the day after the new trial was ordered, and on August 14 there was an attempt to assassinate a defense witness, Maitre Labori. Political upheavals saw resignations of presidents and formations of new cabinets. Dooley reports that "an ex-Prisidint iv Fr-rance come boundin' in, an', r-rushin' up th' steps iv th' thrybune, smacked Gin'ral Merceer in th' eye. Th' gr-reatest rayspict was shown fr th' former chief magistrate iv th' raypublic. No wan shot at him. He was white with rage. 'Th' honor iv Fr-rance is at stake,' he says. 'Our counthry lies prostrate in th' mud.' " He continues, "Whin I saw th' ar-rmy disorganized an' Fr-rance beset be foreign foes, I raysigned. . . . Was I to stay in office, an' have me hat smashed in ivry time I wint out to walk?" The defense of Dreyfus becomes "an exthranyous matther, whin th' honor iv th' ar-rmy is at stake." Ironically, a mysterious lady in white, the divine Sara Bernhardt, overlooks the proceedings like a goddess.

Not only Zola but also the patriotic poet Paul Deroulède was involved in French political activities in 1899, for which Deroulède, in 1900, was banished for ten years. Dooley, beginning the third essay, remarks, "They've arrested a pote. That was all r-right; fr Fr-rance is sufferin' fr'm too much pothry that'll scan, as Hogan says, an' too much morality that won't." The Dreyfus affair brought forth, also, a M. Guérin and a M. Guerin on the basis of which Dooley said Guerin is "an Irish name . . . but this la-ad don't appear to be wan iv us,—Jools Guerin." As chief of the Anti-Semitic League, he had been arrested by the government, but Dooley holds no quarrel with

Guérin's feelings: "They're on'y two known methods iv finance,—bankin' an' burglary. Th' Jews has th' first down fine, but all th' rest iv th' wurruld is at home in th' second." Andre Lebon, the Minister for the Colonies at the time of Dreyfus's confinement on Devil's Island, became known in the foreign press as "the torturer of Dreyfus." His testimony did not improve public opinion of him, and Dooley features his friend Guerin, now editor of an "Anti-Jew" paper, rising to Lebon's defense by calling a five-o'clock revolution at his house and appearing "dhressed fr'm head to foot in Harveyized, bomb-proof steel, with an asbestos rose in his buttonhole."

The chief courtroom events in the second week of the retrial were Bertillon's attack on Dreyfus on August 25 and other witnesses' ridicule of it on August 28. Dooley resumes his report in the fourth essay with "th' air was full iv rumors iv an approachin' massacree." Upon the call for M. Bertillon he responds like Superman, "descindin' fr'm th' roof in a parachute." Bertillon's testimony is reported by Dooley: "Clearly, this letther was written by a Jew. Here I paused, f'r I had no samples iv th' Cap's writin' to compare with it. So I wrote wan mesilf." The means by which he accomplished the forgery inspires the full flight of Dooley's imagination:

I first laid down over th' letther a piece of common tissue paper. Th' writin' was perfectly plain through this. Thin I threw it on a screen eighteen hands high. Thin I threw it off. Thin I set it to music, an' played it on a flute. Thin I cooked it over a slow fire, an' left it in a cool airy place to dhry. In an instant it flashed over me how th' forgery was done. "Th' Cap first give it to his little boy to write. Thin he had his wife copy it in imitation iv Macchew Dhryfuss's handwritin'. This Macchew wrote it in imitation iv Estherhazy. Thin th' Cap had it put on a typewriter, an' r-run through a wringer. Thin he laid it transversely acrost a piece of wall paper; an', whereiver th' key wurrud sponge-cake appeared, he was thereby able f'r to make a sympathetic lesion, acquirin' all th' characteristics iv th' race, an' a dam sight more."

Perhaps the best of Dunne's ability to see both sides of a situation can be found in the fifth essay on the Dreyfus case. Here Dooley tells Hennessy how he would have addressed the court, had he been permitted, as one of "gin-rous confreres iv th' wurruld's press." Even the tormented Captain Dreyfus has by now contradicted himself too often and has had too much public exposure to be regarded as completely innocent. Dooley addresses him in court, "They was a time, Cap, whin 'twas seryously thought iv takin' ye fr'm th' Divvle's Own Island an' makin' ye prisident iv th' Women's Rescue League. But I'm afraid, Cap, ye're disqualified f'r that position be what we've heard fr'm ye'er own lips durin' th' thrile. Ye lost a good job. Thin there ar-re some other things about ye I don't undherstand. I can't make out what ye meant be pretindin' to go to It'ly an' doublin' back into Germany; an' I wish f'r me own peace iv mind all ye'er explanations'd mate." But he sees Dreyfus's problems as mostly endemic to the human race, and turns next to the topic of the French honor, for the French had said, " 'Th' honor iv th' Fr-rinch people an' th' honor iv th' Fr-rinch ar-rmy is on thrile'; and ye've put him in th' dock instead iv th' Cap." Of General Mercier, he concludes, "I'd hate to insure again burglars th' naytional honor that was guarded be that ol' gazabo." There was no pure truth, right, or honor among those involved; and Dooley would dismiss Dreyfus by saying, "Ye may not be a thraitor, but ye're worse. Ye're become a bore," and dismiss the press because, although it is the paladium of our liberties, "our liberties no longer requires a palajeem."

The second court martial found Dreyfus guilty of treason with "extenuating circumstances"; he was pardoned by President Loubet on September 19 of the same year. Not until July of 1903 did both he and Picquart gain reinstatement. Upon Hennessy's accusation that Dooley never set foot in the door of the trial, Dooley reports with clever mixture of the French and Irish that "Mechell Onnessy or Mike Hennessy" whom he talked with at the rolling mills had conversed with him in French through an interpreter. Of the Dreyfus case, Onnessy-Hennessy said "he niver heerd of it" (*Hearts*, 240–85). And so this international event went down in Dooley history.

III   *Burgeoning Internationalism*

Americans with relatives, not merely ancestors, in foreign countries had intimate concern for activities abroad. Thus the nationalists of Greece against the Moslems caused Mr. Dooley to inquire of Hogan's son, "How goes the war between th' ac-cursed infidel an' th' dog iv a Christian?" The son indicates why this essay bears the title "On the Decadence of Greece: " 'Whin I

think iv Leonidas at th' pass iv Thermometer,' he says, 'an' So-
an'-so on th' field iv Marathon an' This-or-That th' Spartan hero,'
he says, 'I cannot undherstand f'r th' life iv me why th' Greeks
shud have been dhruv fr'm pillar to post be an ar-rmy iv slaves.'"
But Dooley sees the conflict in relation to other struggles
between nations and in terms of ethnic conflicts on Archey
Road—whereupon the gas house becomes analogous to the
Acropolis—and in terms of the movement of history. He predicts
for the incredulous Hennessy a time when the Greeks would
have moved out and the Swedes moved into the tenth precinct
(*Peace*, 239–44).

When a delegation from the New York Chamber of Commerce
visited England, Dooley declared he did not know what a
Chamber of Commerce really is, "unless 'tis a place where
business men go to sleep." If this trend continues, his businessman, called Cy, will replace Ambassador Choate with "such
associate diplomats as Higgins th' Machiavelly iv th' dhry goods
thrade, an' Hoontz th' Bismark iv th' pickle industhry" (*Opinions*, 37–42).

The bonds between England and the United States, fortified
by a common language, frequently amused Mr. Dooley. In "On
the Victorian Era," which takes as its topic the celebration of the
queen's diamond jubilee in 1897, Dooley assesses the
accomplishments of passing time; but Hennessy asks with his
usual indignation at Dooley's rhetoric, "What have ye had to do
with all these things?" Mr. Dooley replies, "I had as much to do
with thim as th' queen" (*Peace*, 170–74).

There was a continual need to "cement relationships," a
metaphor Dooley became fond of, especially with England
because of occasional differences such as the boundary dispute
between Venezuela and British Guiana, the Canadian-Alaskan
boundaries, and proposed canal rights in Nicaragua. In "International Amenities" Dooley continued the topic of cementing
efforts of "Amateur Ambassadors" and spoke of "an outburst iv
devotion to th' ol' land fr'm which our fathers sprung or was
sprung be th' authorities." The English still regard the Americans
as savages, however, asking at a diplomatic gathering, "what
tribe did ye say they belonged to? Soos?" The "Star-Spangled
Banner," Lord Cheesehop declares, is "th' on'y Indyan music I
iver heerd" (*Observations*, 33–37). British manners and royalty,
and Americans' desire to emulate them, reappeared in 1901 with

"King Edward's Coronation" (*Observations*, 131–38).

In "Immigration," Dooley's doubletalk presents the view of the American admitting he arrived as an immigrant but preferring to keep other immigrants out, saying the attitude is that "th' Goddess iv Liberty 'll meet thim at th' dock with an axe in her hand." But since our country has not fulfilled the promise it offers to the "anarchists" forced to leave other countries, Dooley wisely recommends the best way to reduce the numbers immigrating is to "teach thim all about our instichoochions befure they come" (*Observations*, 49–54).

America's new eminence in world affairs following the Spanish-American War was recognized by gestures from other countries soon after Roosevelt became president; the Kaiser conferred a medal on the president, and sent his brother Prince Henry on a good-will tour of the United States. Dooley in "Prince Henry's Visit" remains skeptical about the duties of an emperor but admits that the emperor's brother "has more wurruk thin a bartinder in a prohibition town." In "Prince Henry's Reception," he said, "A prince is a gr-reat man in th' ol' counthry, but he niver is as gr-reat over there as he is here" (*Observations*, 73–88).

Like the essay on "Immigration," Dooley's thoughts on "Cuba vs. Beet Sugar" have lasting effectiveness, for the attitudes and the problems seem never to change as time passes. Explaining that "we freed Cubia but we didn't free annything she projooces," he grows expansive on the problems of hunger and the Americans' awakening to the fact that their own sugar sales would be threatened by import. He says, "A sort iv cravin' come over her that it was hard to tell fr'm th' same feelin' iv vacancy that she knew whin she was opprissed be th' Hated Casteel. Hunger, Hinnissy, is about th' same thing in a raypublic as in a dispotism." He cleverly adapts the sayings of many people, including his own, to defense of the Beet: "Th' constichoochion follows th' Beet ex propria vigore, as Hogan says. . . . An' so, Hinnissy, we put th' pie back into th' ice-chest where we keep our honor an' ginerosity an' lock th' dure an' Cubia goes home, free an' hopeless" (*Observations*, 91–94).

"I see be th' pa-apers" on one occasion ("The King in his Shirt-Sleeves") led Mr. Dooley to speculate how long the kings of the world can "stand havin' all these things known about thim," inspired by the actions of the King of Belgium, whose daughter chose to marry someone not her equal. As soon as the king's private life becomes known and he looks like the rest of us, his subjects will no longer tolerate his being king (*Dissertations*, 318). The Austro-Hungarian heir married beneath him but found his wife not permitted to sit with him except on military occasions (on their anniversary, June 28, 1914, they were shot in Sarajevo). In "Royal Doings," Dooley returned to his topic, concentrating on the romance of the elderly Sophie of the Hapsburgs. Dooley says, " 'Tis sthrange how manny ladies with wan leg in th' grave wud like to see th' other in th' front row iv th' chorus" (*Dissertations*, 11–15). "Our Representatives Abroad" discussed the decline in power of the ambassador, but Dooley found recognition somewhat restored in "Diplomatic Uniforms," when Charlemagne Tower as ambassador to Russia solved the problem of being mistaken for a waiter. Dooley says, "Th' name itsilf is unyform enough. Some names sounds like overalls; some sounds like a long coat an' a high hat, but Charleymayne Tower sounds like th' clothes a boss knights timplar wears ivry three years. It has forty pounds iv epaulets on its shoulders" (*Dissertations*, 97–104). After he acquires his new uniform, to suit the name, the Czar says, "Nay, Charleymayne, kneei not to me in thim pants on this flure. Rather shud I kneel to thee, f'r niver since king an' tailor jined together to rule th' wurruld, has human legs been encased in so happy a pair iv bloomers."

"An International Police Force" takes up much serious history, recounting the Czar of Russia's invitation in 1899 to nations to confer on disarmament at The Hague, and the "bad charackter" of Cipriano Castro, dictator of Venezuela, who had refused to settle the claims of foreigners in his country but who accepted the reduction of the Hague Tribunal from $40 million to $8 million. Dooley cannot be misled by moderate success, however, and expects little from such a body: "There's th' internaytional coort, ye say, but I say where ar-re th' polis?" But then he sagely perceives that if such a police force existed it would function as in real life. "All th' biggest crooks wud get on th' polis foorce" (*Dissertations*, 161–66).

One of the best essays Dunne wrote on monarchies, entitled "Turkish Politics," followed the Armenian Massacre and resultant political upheaval. It continues his previous assertion that monarchs must keep themselves removed from public life so that the public does not know how common they are, and in it Dooley disclaims any intention of aspiring to the job of royalty. He sees

that the real problem is the attitude and bearing which a
monarch is bred to, and his remarks remain valid:

What can ye expict fr'm a man that niver was taught annything betther
thin that he cud do annything he wanted to do without bein' called
down f'r it? It doesn't make anny diff'rence whether 'tis a polisman or
th' Rajah iv Beloochistan, be gorry, put a club in his hand an' tell him
that he can use it an' he'll begin usin' it tomorrah. He'll break wan head
tomorrah, two th' next day, an' befure he's been on th' foorce or th'
throne a year it'll be a whack on th' chimbly befure he says "How ar-re
ye." By an' by he'll get so manny people afraid iv him that he'll be in
danger and that'll make him afraid iv thim, an' thin he'll be more
dangerous thin iver, d'ye mind? Th' on'y man ye need to be afraid iv is
th' man that's afraid iv ye. An' that's what makes a tyrant." (Says,
214–26)

   One of the last essays Dunne wrote, for *Liberty* magazine in
1926, was "Mr. Dooley on Mussolini." Again, as he had managed
with German or Dutch and French, he now combines Italian with
his own brand of English for bilingual puns; also, he gives a
history of Fascism and of Mussolini's rise to power, connecting
with common practices in the great classical age of Rome, not
forgetting to comment on Mussolini's famous fictional statement
that he made the trains run on time, a statement Dooley
disbelieves: "Flaherty tells me they don't say what hour a thrain
will come in but what month. Ye go down to th' deepo to meet th'
May 30th and th' fellow with th' migaphone hollers out: 'Thrain
forty-two, doo on May 30th, will ar-rive Janooary 1st on thrack
ilivan, p'r'aps.' " In keeping with his talent for seeing both sides
of a question, Dooley summarizes the glories of Italy to show
what its patriots appreciate. In a fine essay with much of history
and tradition as well as humor, Dooley explains that heroes and
martyrs are not those who go out of this life on a dose of castor
oil; and he implies that Mussolini will not be one of the great men
of history: "Thim that take up th' soord shall perish be th' soord.
An' I s'pose that goes f'r th' casthor-ile bottle too" (*Liberty*,
March 27, 1926).

IV   *Americans at Home*

   The farflung empire of Dooley's opinions extended northward
to Alaska gold-seeking (*Peace*, 100–104) and to the North Pole,

where he followed the adventures of the Norwegian arctic explorer Fridtjof Nansen (*Peace*, 192-96) and later those of Evelyn Briggs Baldwin and Admiral Robert Peary. Peary made his fifth voyage in 1905 and 1906, when Dooley concluded that, personally, he would leave "Th' Pole f'r th' polars," by which he meant the Eskimos should do the exploring. Peary reached the North Pole on his sixth voyage in 1909 (*Observations*, 203-10).

While Americans were busy extending themselves beyond their boundaries, however, they failed to regard as Americans those living at home, namely the Indians and the blacks. For the beleaguered Indian, Dooley suggests a balloon or a diving bell in the Pacific Ocean as his only recourse, given the attitudes of the white man, who regards anyone else as a savage. From a feeling of superiority, the white man says, "I'd be civilized, if I hadn't on so much as a bangle bracelet," but the Indian is not civilized even if he wears ten pairs of pants (*Peace*, 245-48). And just as with much sympathy for the Indian Dooley suggested that Hennessy, to improve his outlook, go and enlist as an Indian, in "The Negro Problem" he tackled the failures of the Fourteenth Amendment. His black friend whom he calls "Snowball" with much intelligence and altruism becomes a lawyer, only to be defeated by the social structure, then to turn to journalism in "Th' Colored Supplimint"; but, finding public taste running toward the "quadhroon publications," he has to admit defeat there. A series of attempts and failures makes him realize his race has a chance only in running crap games; and he asks his old abolitionist friend, Dooley, to drop in someday. Hennessy expresses the smug conservative view: "Well, they got to take their chances. Ye can't do annything more f'r thim than make thim free." Dooley agrees: "Ye can't; on'y whin ye tell thim they're free they know we're on'y sthringin' thim" (*Philosophy*, 217-22). In addition to "The Booker Washington Incident," about Theodore Roosevelt's inviting the black man to lunch at the White House, Dunne wrote "The Race Question," in which he gives a concise summary of Reconstruction and connects it with the White House incident. The problem with Roosevelt's idea to "glad-hand" the black man "up to a higher plane" is that "th' higher ye boost th' naygur be askin' him up to th' White House, th' farther he has to fall whin he gets about two blocks south iv th' White House." Yet Dooley manages to make his suggestion of interracial marriage sound not like a fear but like an ideal (*Dissertations*, 185-90).

Reform frequently gained Dunne's attention, but his Dooley was always skeptical of the motives and probable accomplishments of anything calling itself by that name. In "On Reform Candidates," he deplored the intent of reformers to overlook anything good around them—anything "but the pest-house an' the bridewell." While the moneyed interests discuss reform, Dooley's friend Flanagan, a poor man, wins an election by being active and visible among the people (*Peace*, 111-17). Distinguishing reformers and politicians, he said, "Rayformers, Hinnissy, is in favor iv suppressin' ivrything, but rale pollyticians believes in suppressin' nawthin' but ividince" (*Opinions*, 171-77). He characterized the Populists as having for their principles "Anny ol' thing that th' other pa-arties has rijected" and repeats his friend Cassiday's report on their disorderly convention, where the delegates sing "Pa-pa Cleveland's Teeth Are Filled with Goold" and eject a man for wearing a coat (*Peace*, 197-201). In "Reform Administration," Dooley offered a variation of his opinion that reform goes contrary to the grain and provided a history of "reform" once it is elected to office. He says, "In th' first place 'tis a gr-reat mistake to think that annywan r-aly wants to rayform. Ye niver heerd iv a man rayformin' himsilf. He'll rayform other people gladly. He likes to do it. But a healthy man'll niver rayform while he has th' strength." When the reform candidate gets elected, he becomes puffed up with self-concern: "He thinks you an' me, Hinissy, has been watchin' his spotless career f'r twenty years, that we've read all he had to say. . . . So th' minyit he gets into th' job he begins a furyous attimpt to convart us into what we've been thryin' not to be iver since we come into th' wurruld." The reformer naively thinks that "business an' honesty is th' same thing . . . because they dhress alike" and puts into office those who express fine sentiments while vice and crime enjoy a boom. When dishonesty returns to office, the system returns to normal and functions with its relative efficiency. The reformer "spinds th' rest iv his [civilian] life tellin' us where we are wrong. He's good at that. On'y he don't undherstand that people wud rather be wrong an' comfortable thin right in jail" (*Observations*, 167-72).

Likewise suspicious of anarchists, he put in familiar homelike terms the political upheavals of Europe. In Chicago anarchists were mostly against policemen, but his cousin Terence's family began to "rasp on wan another" until Father Kelly visited and called a plumber. "Arnychists," said Mr. Dooley, "is sewer gas" (*Peace*, 229–33). In "The Ruling Class," his anarchist Casey "whales away" with a lecture demanding of his hearers whether they are slaves until his little German wife appears, calls him a blackguard, and ends his public career; in like manner the ruling class controls its radicals (*Hearts*, 165–69). In "Doings of Anarchists," Dooley reiterated his opinion that kings should keep themselves from the commoners in order to preserve their respect; and he describes anarchists as "down on th' polis foorce an' in favor iv th' pop'lace, an' whin they've kilt a king they call on th' polis to save thim fr'm th' mob." He recognizes also the desire for attention: "If they was no newspapers they'd be few arnychists. They want to get their pitchers in th' pa-apers an' they can't do it be wheelin' bananas through th' sthreets or milkin' a cow, so they go out an' kill a king" (*Philosophy*, 195–200).

In 1894 the Lexow Committee investigated police corruption in New York city, but in talking about Lexow, Dooley saw that reformers seek to drive others out of high places so that they can take over and profit from established corruption (*Hearts*, 35–40). In "A Brand from the Burning," Dooley relates the career of one Flanagan, who used sheer physical brutality to boss a canal gang and then entered politics, making money from real estate, which "includes near ivrything fr'm vagrancy to manslaughter." The priest who opposed Flanagan as immoral now turns to support him for paying off the church debt; and Flanagan moves out of ward politics into city politics, only to disdain to help a former friend and save a brand from the burning which he himself deserves (*Hearts*, 66–71).

Dooley remained consistently opposed to moneyed interests, especially those such as Rockefeller and Carnegie who took money from the poor and then attempted to buy grace by establishing public museums and libraries. Dooley's personal acquaintance with poverty on Archey Road showed him that the poor needed food and health care, not art works. "When the Trust Is at Work" begins with his observation of a passing funeral, that of a poor man who worked under the odors of the Armour meat packing plant and whose few relatives after the funeral straggled home "in th' dust to th' empty panthry an' the' fireless grate." Dooley claims he has no word to say against those who "sets back in their own house an' lot an' makes th' food iv th' people dear," even though "they tilt the price iv beef to where wan pound iv it costs as much as manny th' man in this Ar-rchey Road 'd wurrk fr'm th' risin' to th' settin' iv th' sun to get."He says "ivry cint a pound manes a new art musoom or a new church, to take th' edge off hunger" (*Hearts*, 61-65).

In "Mr. Carnegie's Gift," actually ten million dollars to a university in Scotland, Dooley would, had he the money to give, "endow a bar'l iv oatmeal fr ivry boy in Scotland that wanted an idjacation," because "Idjacation can always be had, but they'se niver enough oatmeal in Scotland." In the role of Andrew Carnegie, he says, "I've got into th' habit iv makin' it, but not into th' habit iv spindin' it. I can't buy things with it, fr there's nawthin' I've larned how to buy that won't make money fr me. I can't give it to th' poor because if they had it they wudden't be poor anny longer." On the idea that opportunity knocks for everyone, he says, "Th' poor ar-re people that've been out at wurruk whin opporchunity knocked"; and Carnegie's gift to education will teach others how to follow in his footsteps, how to loot. Father Kelly disagrees, saying that education means work and worry, and defends Andrew Carnegie for his achievements. Dooley admits he can see the validity of Father Kelly's viewpoint: "Men that wants it [education] 'll have it be hook an' be crook, an' thim that don't ra-aly want it niver will get it. Ye can lade a man up to th' university, but ye can't make him think" (*Opinions*, 145-50). It calls to mind Plunkitt of Tammany, who became a millionaire and said "I seen my opportunities and I took 'em."

Carnegie's disapproval of Homer provides Dooley a grand opportunity to satirize his differences with Carnegie, especially because Homer wrote libraries instead of building them. Carnegie knows that Achilles acts nothing like a king, for he has personal acquaintance with King Edward as evidence. Dooley agrees with Carnegie on one point, that the illustrations of Homer's kings show them all to be truckmen: "Yes, sir, ivry king iv thim was dhrivin' a dhray an' fightin' fr'm it just like ye see thim on th' docks." Concerned with Hogan's reaction to Carnegie's exposure of his favorite poet, however, Dooley considers that Hogan will have the good sense to say "Homer don't care" (*Dissertations*, 145-50).

Dooley consistently believed that Andrew Carnegie's charity

was both misplaced and intended for self-advertisement. The proliferation of Carnegie libraries without books to fill them he saw as foolish and burdensome in the form of taxation: "A Carnaygie libry is a large, brown-stone, impenethrible buildin' with th' name iv th' maker blown on th' dure. Libry, fr'm th' Greek wurruds, libus, a book, an' ary, sildom,—sildom a book. A Carnaygie libry is archytechoor, not lithrachoor." But literature will be represented on the buildings with the names of the most celebrated dead authors painted on the walls alternating with Carnegie's name: "Th' live authors will stand outside an' wish they were dead." Impersonating Carnegie he dares to say that "Th' worst thing ye can do f'r anny man is to do him good," and for Dooley doing right means distribution of food to the poor. Carnegie maintains that "Th' way to abolish poverty an' bust crime is to put up a brown-stone buildin' in ivry town in th' counthry with me name over it." In return for a $50,000 library, the town must raise $1 million "to maintain th' buildin' an' keep me name shiny." Dooley simply refuses to accept that libraries maintain literature, saying, "Libries niver encouraged lithrachoor anny more thin tombstones encourage livin'" but he advocates instead of buildings a system of subsidy for the poets. In one respect he agrees with Carnegie, that gifts should be noticeable, and he admits that when he throws the coin in the church collection plate he hurls it so hard from about two yards away that Father Kelly must turn to see who did it (*Dissertations*, 177–82).

Much funnier is Dooley's disapproval of Carnegie's Hero Fund for heroes in the daily walks of life, excluding "sojers, polismen, an' invistors." He gives an example of the medal struck with Carnegie's name in huge letters, and himself as hero having saved Hennessy from the Illinois and Michigan Canal "f'river doomed to be a sandwich man an' parade th' sthreets advartisin' th' gin'rosity an' noble charakter iv Andhrew Carnaygie." Hennessy's children thereafter would have to bring Dooley birthday presents and Hennessy would have to lend him money. Dooley tells about Clancy saved by Muggins and hounded by Muggins for the rest of his life, concluding that he would be saved by a fireman or a policeman but never let an amateur hero near him (*Dissertations*, 293–99).

Industrialists set no example for the multitude, and Dooley finds corruption so rampant that in "High Finance" he determines to buy some stock because "they're goin' to hur-rl th' chairman iv th' comity into jail. That's what th' pa-apers calls a ray iv hope in th' clouds iv dipression that've covered th' market so long." When his friend Cassidy lost on a money-making venture with this chairman, Dooley told him he was up against haut finance, not burglary nor obtaining money under false pretenses and not manslaughter but "a judicious seliction fr'm th' best features iv thim ar-rts" (*Philosophy,* 155-60).

In "On Wall Street," Dooley says that "whin business gets above sellin' tinpinny nails in a brown paper cornucopy, 'tis hard to tell it fr'm murther." The essay features "Scaldy Harriman" and "Scrappy Morgan" bragging about their respective endeavors, with Morgan saying, "I've jined th' mountains iv th' moon railway with th' canals iv Mars, an' I'll be haulin' wind fr'm the caves iv Saturn befure th' first iv th' year." Tim Mangan, the bootblack at the Alhambra Hotel, invests during the boom and loses all his money in the ensuing depression (*Opinions,* 189-95). Banks baffle Mr. Dooley with their unwillingness to take his small sum of eighty-five dollars as savings deposit while they lend a thousand to a poor risk, but he decides that the only ones who can be buncoed are the smart people, for they try to bunco: "A man that buys a goold brick thinks he is swindlin' a poor Indyan that don't know its value" (*Dissertations,* 303-308). Dooley explains panics according to what he has read, that if people do not take their money out of the banks, everything will be all right; thus he reflects the attitude of economic leaders in the Panic of 1907 (*Says,* 159-66).

In "The Crusade Against Vice," Dooley says that "th' more ye see it th' betther ye like it [vice]." The reformers who use the crusade to acquire votes eventually find that flagging business motivates them to support vice. Dooley concludes, "I'm afraid . . . that th' frinds iv vice is too sthrong in this wurruld iv sin f'r th' frinds iv varchue. Th' good man, th' crusader, on'y wurruks at th' crusade wanst in five years, an' on'y whin he has time to spare fr'm his other jooties. 'Tis a pastime f'r him. But th' definse iv vice is a business with th' other la-ad an' he nails away at it, week days an' Sundays, holy days an' fish days, mornin', noon an' night" (*Opinions,* 153-58).

In "The Labor Troubles," Dooley finds that everything has joined the unions, including Hogan's hens, of which "wan iv thim laid an egg two days in succession an' th' others sthruck, th' rule iv th' union bein' that no hen shall lay more eggs thin th' most reluctant hen in th' bunch." Unions have even held up funeral processions to check for union cards, while working hours—with the old system upset—are increased for some types of workers and decreased for others. Dooley, deploring the loss of the old system when Labor and Capital worked hand in hand, says, "Capital still pats Labor on th' back, but on'y with an axe. Labor rayfuses to be threated as a frind. It wants to be threated as an inimy. It thinks it gets more that way." But he, as independent bartender, gets crushed between the two (*Dissertations*, 59–64).

Strikers earn little sympathy from Dooley, for a strike is a working man's vacation, he says, and, moreover, "Sthrikes come in th' summer time an' lockouts in th' winter." Some people, such as farmers, cannot go on strike; and they have Dooley's sympathy (*Says*, 78–88).

Self-interest guides most American endeavors, including that of the New York Custom House, where Dooley's friend Hannigan found his dreams of bringing gifts back from Ireland destroyed by officers protecting their own interests. Angrily retaliating with the remark that they forgot to remove his tattoo, he finds himself arrested for smuggling foreign art (*Opinions*, 161–67). Later, Nelson W. Aldrich of Rhode Island, a multi-millionaire industrialist, headed the Senate Committee on Finance and acted exactly as Hannigan had experienced. The Payne Tariff Bill had been intended to revise tariffs downward, and did so with some insignificant items; but its 800-some amendments in 1909 actually increased the average rate on dutiable goods by about 1 percent. Dooley reports reading a copy of the bill and delivers one of his best satires naming the free items: "Ye haven't got a thing on ye'er back excipt ye'er skin . . . I haven't got as far as th' hide schedule yet." Free items that Dooley finds are one's own teeth, sea moss, bird seed, joss sticks, and opium. He concludes with a sample of the prolonged debate, conducted in polite but scathing terms, with the Senator from Virginia, for example, saying, "I wud be foorced to waive me almost insane prejudice again th' hellish docthrines iv th' distinguished sinitor fr'm Rhode Island" (*Says*, 144–57).

Dooley makes throughout his speeches numerous references to his "frind Jawn D." and in "The Big Fine" he finds that John D. Rockefeller has been caught at last for "exeedin' th' speed limit in acquirin' money." Rockefeller had been handed a fine of

$29,240,000 when Judge Kenesaw Mountain Landis in April 1907 had found the Standard Oil Company of New Jersey guilty on 1,462 counts of obtaining rebates from the Chicago and Alton Railroad. Dooley said Rockefeller had announced himself as "a custojeen iv money appinted be himsilf" and that "he's a kind iv a society f'r th' previntion of croolty to money." Further, Dooley now says, an appeal "is where ye ask wan coort to show it's contempt f'r another coort." Of the decision, Dooley says, "Th' on'y wan that bows to th' decision is th' fellow that won, an' pretty soon he sees he's made a mistake, f'r wan day th' other coort comes out an' declares that th' decision of th' lower coort is another argymint in favor iv abolishing night law schools." Dooley sees Rockefeller facing the fine or "fifty-eight millyon days" in jail and also puts the fine in commoner's terms of equaling "Three millyon dhrunk an' disorderly cases" (*Says*, 158–67). As Dooley suspected when the appeal was in process, Rockefeller paid never a cent; the decision was reversed the next year.

The year 1906 made prominent the investigative powers of lawyer Charles Evans Hughes into the conduct of the New York life-insurance companies with "one executive testifying," as George E. Mowry writes, "that his company alone had spent close to a million dollars in five years stopping 'undesirable legislation' "[2] The companies became known as free speculators of their clients' funds, both crooked and wasteful, and freely mixing politics and business. This essay may well be Dooley's most complicated discourse, even though he resorts as usual to the tactic of placing it in the perspective of an Archey Road acquaintance. Beginning with the statement that the newspapers often call for business to "swab out our govermint with business methods," he adds that this means that "We must injooce th' active, conscientious young usurers f'rm Wall Sthreet to take an inthrest in public affairs." The result becomes a Herculean task requiring religious devotion: "Oh, f'r a Moses to lead us out of th' wilderness an' clane th' Augeenyan stables" but "Where is Moses? . . . this all-around Moses, soldier, sailor, locksmith, doctor, stable-boy, polisman, an' disinfectant?" He calls upon the Honorable Ephraim Duck, author of numerous works proclaiming his name, to act in place of Moses, but Duck is down in Springfield, "doin' a little ligislative law business f'r th' gas comp'ny." The judge Dooley refers to as "our most illusthrees life-insurance solicitor . . . in th' wurruld."

When Dooley's friend John Cassiday exposes such corruption as the buying of city streets, he says, "We may be a tough gang over at th' City Hall. . . . But, thank th' Lord, no man iver accused us iv bein' life-insurance prisidints." Through the usual maze of double talk actually exposing the crime, Cassiday concludes, "In time, I hope to see th' same honesty, good faith, an' efficiency in th' Life Insurance Comp'nies an' th' Thrusts that we see now in th' administhration iv Tammany Hall" (*Dissertations,* 275–81).

The varied legal entanglements which concerned Mr. Dooley have been mostly gathered in Edward Bander's *Mr. Dooley on the Choice of Law* (1968) with an introduction by Roscoe Pound. "On Expert Testimony" reports a debate on the trial of Adolph Leutgert in 1897. Leutgert was an owner of a Chicago sausage factory, suspected of (and later convicted for) murdering his wife and grinding up her remains in the food. Dooley parodies the testimony concerning the size of the vat and a professor's experiments with dissolving human hair, factors which will have little bearing on the decision of the jury, whose three questions are "Did Lootgert look as though he'd kill his wife? Did his wife look as though she ought to be kilt? Isn't it time we wint to supper?" (*Peace,* 141–45). In "Hanging Aldermen," Dooley explains how a bribe works through appealing to several sensitivities until the victim yields; but Dooley reveals his characteristic opposition to business. The bribed alderman "was expelled fr'm th' St. Vincent de Pauls, an' ilicted a director iv a bank th' same day" (*Hearts,* 22–29).

In "Cross-examinations," Dooley tells how he attempted to act as witness for the prosecution and found himself accused: "I was two minyits givin' me tistymony, an' two hours thryin' to convince th' hon'rable coort—a loafer be th' name iv Duffy—an' th' able jury that I hadn't stolen th' shirt on me back fr'm a laundhry wagon. Th' coort was goin' to confine me in jail f'r life f'r contimpt, th' lawyer f'r th' definse sthrongly intimated that I was in th' neighborhood whin Charlie Ross was kidnapped an' th' jury ast to be allowed to bring in a verdict iv manslaughter again me without exthra pay." He then recounts the suit of a dismissed valet against his former employer in which the employer's wife is found guilty of dying her hair, a process revealing that jurors are more vengeful against women than against men (*Opinions,* 117–22).

"The Law's Delays" introduces a stay of proceedings which Dooley defines as the device "be which th' high coorts keep in form." Thereafter the convicted murderer languishes in prison while the years pass and the relatives forget him, until the court decides "that th' verdict was conthry to th' law an' th' ividence." Dooley would like to be a judge, "dhreamin' th' happy hours away" because he knows he can sleep anywhere (*Observations,* 15–19).

Dunne's "Expert Testimony" Edward J. Bander retitles "Insanity as a Defense or the M'Naghten Rule in a Nutshell."[3] Dooley defines an expert witness as a "doctor that thinks a man must be crazy to be rich" and sets up an example of Hennessy's stealing a watch from Hogan in order to make himself rich. Hogan becomes known as not the proper man to have the care of a watch; and a doctor testifies that Hennessy, though perfectly sane all his life, experienced temporary insanity because "so much sanity wint to his head an' blew th' cover off." After Dooley finishes his report of the trial, Hennessy inquires, "What's th' diff-rence between that kind iv tistymony an' perjury?" Dooley replies, "Ye pay ye're money an' take ye're choice" (*Says,* 168–79).

"On Making a Will" provided Dooley the opportunity to construct one of his insightful definitions: "To be injyeable a will must be at wan an' th' same time a practical joke on th' heirs an' an advertisemint iv the man that made it," or what Hogan calls "th' last infirmary" of the noble mind. Dock O'Leary's prescription for aged millionaires, after everything else fails, consists of advice that they alter their wills (*Will,* 3–16).

The most famous of Dunne's legal writing, however, was "The Supreme Court Decisions," in which he characterizes the Court: "It's old an' it's feeble an' it prefers to set on th' front stoop an' amuse th' childer. It wudden't last a minyit in thim thropical climes. 'Twud get a pain in th' fourteenth amindmint an' die befure th' doctors cud get ar-round to cut it out." As Bander points out,

The case involved, Downes v. Bidwell 182 U.S. 244 (1901), must be read for full appreciation of a less than grand style of legal writing, aptly termed by John P. Frank in his "Marble Palace" as "legal massive." Those who are familiar with James M. Marsh's use of the Dooley method in his satire "Mr. Dooley discovers a Unanimous Dissent," 62 Case & Comment No. 6, 8 (1957), can see it is still an effective approach. It is interesting to note that Downes v. Bidwell was one of a series of cases popularly known as the "insular cases" among which was one called Dooley v. U.S., which may well have inspired the entire piece as there is intrinsic evidence in the satire that Dunne had read it.[4]

The civil rights of Cubans had been left, by the agreement of cession, for determination by Congress, and Congress levied a special tariff against Puerto Rican imports. Further, in keeping with the 1900 election as a victory for imperialists, the Supreme Court in 1901 decided not to interfere in the doings of Congress. Dooley phrases the popular question in the words of "Mary's Little Lamb": "Some fellow said that ivrywhere th' constitution wint, th' flag was sure to go," but he concludes that the Court follows the election returns, and concedes that the Constitution had no business "to shadow the flag to all th' tough resorts on th' Passyfic Coast" (*Opinions*, 21–26).

At the turn of the century anything gold suggested political position, whether in the form of the president's cat or the "gold-headed cane" with which the Court understood that the Constitution walks. Dooley had already discussed "The Currency Question" at the Chicago level with several persons in his pub (*Peace*, 175–80). In "On Political Parades" Hennessy arrives wearing the colors of the opposition—a silver-painted hat and a silver cape—to show his hatred of capital (*Peace*, 181–86).

Those interested in McKinley politics can follow "my frind Mack's" career through several essays: "A Candidate's Pillory," with every fault exposed to public view; "The Day after the Victory"; "A Visit to Jekyl Island" with Mark Hanna; "Making a Cabinet"; and "Prosperity," which was considered to travel with McKinley against the other great issue known as "humanity" (*Hearts*, 107–79). Dunne considered also the exigencies of Platform Making with "Billy Bryan" denouncing and deploring whatever the Republicans proposed (*Philosophy*, 97–102) and focused on Kentucky politics in two essays (*Philosophy*, 121–28, 181–87). "Troubles of a Candidate" reviews the mudslinging evident in the McKinley versus Bryan campaign, and Dooley, weary of all of it, asks, "Did ye iver notice how much th'

candydates looks alike, an' how much both iv thim looks like
Lydia Pinkham?" (*Philosophy*, 229–34). In "Discusses Party
Politics," he considered the failure of the Democrats to find a
winning presidential candidate (*Opinions*, 93–98) and in
"Fame," the career of loser William Jennings Bryan (*Opinions*,
109–113).

In several places Dooley notes how geographic stereotypes
have restricted much American progress. In "Bad Men from the
West" he opts for "Tarantula Jake, th' whirlwind iv Zuma Pass"
but knows his opposition in the Senator from Massachusetts,
"where human life is held so cheap that no wan thinks iv takin'
it." In defiance, he constructs a very entertaining Wild West
examination for the superintendent of the Smithsonian Institute
(*Observations*, 97–103). "The Fighting Word" concerns a
dispute between Bailey of Texas and Beveridge of Indiana
(*Observations*, 149–54). In "Swearing" Dunne defends
Roosevelt for the historic words he spoke to a trolley man, a "jim
of emotion an' thought come sthraight fr'm th' heart an' wint
right to th' heart. That's wan reason I think a lot iv us likes Tiddy
Rosenfelt that wudden't iver be suspected iv votin' f'r him"
(*Observations*, 223–28).

Dunne's (and hence Dooley's) politics greatly favored Theodore Roosevelt, however, even though Dunne remained a
staunch Democrat. "Youth and Age" denounces the popular
theory that Roosevelt was too young to govern, about which
Dooley said, "I'm old enough to look down on Prisidint Tiddy if I
didn't look up to him" (*Opinions*, 181–86).

In addition to the Roosevelt essays in Dunne's eight collections, Louis Filler in *The World of Mr. Dooley* (1962) reproduces
one entitled "T. R.," which lists a day's activities at Roosevelt's
home at Oyster Bay, to which Dunne was frequently invited, and
another not in dialect called "Good-by, Teddy," which Dunne
wrote for the *American* when Roosevelt left public office in
1909. That Roosevelt upheld many of Dunne's ideals can be seen
through several of Dunne's statements about his friend; for
example, "In one case he had to urge the criminal prosecution of
a man for whose political support he was deeply grateful, and
who had dined at his table."[5]

In "The Intellectual Life," Dooley attacks the idea that
common citizens have no political sense, saying, "Me opinyon iv
pollyticks, if ye shud ask me f'r it, is that we might as well give up

th' experimint. A govermint founded be an ol' farmer like George Wash'nton an' a job-printer like Bin Franklin was bound to go down in roon" (*Dissertations*, 107–12). He called the office of vice-president the next highest to president and the lowest: "It isn't a crime exactly. Ye can't be sint to jail f'r it, but it's a kind iv a disgrace. It's like writin' anonymous letters" (*Dissertations*, 115–20).

In "The Candidate," Dooley presents a statewide assessment of party preferences and the way publicity makes heroes of ordinary persons with ordinary virtues: "A man expicts to be ilicted Prisidint iv th' United States, Hinnissy, f'r th' fine qualities that th' r-rest iv us use on'y to keep out iv th' pinitinchry" (*Dissertations*, 199–203). In "Senatorial Courtesy," he denounces polite speech which permits ignoring all vital issues (*Dissertations*, 193–95); and in "Socialism" he offers a variation on the usual format, setting up this one as a drama with Mr. Larkin advancing the ideals for the others assembled in Dooley's pub: "Th' first thing we'd do wud be to take all th' money in th' wurruld an' throw it into th' lake," and, later, "Thin we'd set ivry wan to wurruk at something." Dooley, as usual when confronted with high-flown ideals, remains practical and objective (*Dissertations*, 265–72).

V   *Women and Family*

Although Dooley remained a confirmed bachelor, his friends and his friends' children and Father Kelly's parishioners brought their domestic problems to him. A soft word, a keen observation, an analogy established with another of his acquaintances who faced a similar problem—all endeared him to Dunne's readers. As in "On Criminals," about the Scanlon boy's "bein' sint down th' short r-road f'r near a lifetime" in spite of his parents' efforts to give him a proper bringing up, so also in "On Paternal Duty" Dooley reassures Hennessy that parents can often do little to secure the love of their children (*Peace*, 118–23). Something occasionally shows up in human nature that no parent can account for. "The Idle Apprentice" tells the story of Jack Carey, born into a household of a drunken father and a mother who was scrubbing floors downtown "where Dennehy got her," and Carey's life of crime ended in a gun battle with the police (*Hearts*, 96–100). "The Soft Spot" describes a miser landlord who rescued a baby girl from a burning house and paid for her upbringing while continuing to make lives miserable for his tenants; Dooley says, "beneath ivry man's outside coat there lies some good feelin'" (*Hearts*, 196–201). "The Tragedy of the Agitator" tells about a father and a son who worked together as scow unloaders until a strike by the union divided them (*Hearts*, 82–84).

One of Dunne's funniest concoctions, "The Bringing Up of Children," provides a delightful change of pace. Dooley comments that one of the sources of his popularity in the ward is that he makes a bluff of adoring children, even though "I'd as lave salute a dish-rag as a recent infant." His visit to Hogan's first child means that he has to scrub off all microbes before approaching the presence, "a toothless ol' gintleman who was settin' up in a cradle atin' his right foot." Hogan delivers a lecture on the new, sanitary methods of rearing children, all of which Dooley, in relating the story to Hennessy, counters point by point. When Hennessy, father of eleven (all of whom, by the way, have names like Patrick Sarsfield and Robert Emmet so that they sound like a roll call of Irish history), scornfully remarks, "Ye know a lot about it," Mr. Dooley replies, "I do. Not bein' an author, I'm a gr-reat critic" (*Dissertations*, 51–55).

"On the Necessity of Modesty Among the Rich" begins with a society ball which calls to Dooley's mind the life and death of a rack-renting Irish landlord who was killed after a big party by a tenant who, driven out of his home with his baby in his arms, ambushed the rich man (*Peace*, 158–64). He tells about his own family reunion, which ended in a fight (*Peace*, 202–207), and a Vanderbilt marrying the Duke of Marlborough (*Peace*, 208–12). Later Dunne wrote about the less-than-peaceful home life of the wealthy (*Will*, 47–54).

Several essays concern the position of woman in both the home and society. Molly Donahue sets the pace by describing the new woman, free from the oppression of man: "She'll wurruk out her own way, without help or hinderance. She'll wear what clothes she wants, an' she'll be no man's slave. They'll be no such thing as givin' a girl in marredge to a clown an' makin' her dipindant on his whims. Th' women'll earn their own livin'; an' mebbe th' men'll stay at home an' dredge in th' house wurruk." Donahue listens quietly but the next morning announces that he is staying at home and the women can go to work in the mill. They quickly relent (*Peace*, 136-40). But the indulgent father buys his progressive daughter a bicycle with which she startles the neighborhood by riding it in a divided skirt. The horrified father asks Father Kelly to say a "pather an' avy quick" but Father Kelly says quietly, " 'Molly,' he says, 'ye look well on that there bicycle,' he says. 'But 'tis th' first time I ever knowed ye was bow-legged' " (*Hearts*, 154-57).

Dunne's essay on polygamy defines a Mormon as "a man that has th' bad taste an' th' rellijion to do what a good manny other men ar-re resthrained fr'm doin' be conscientious scruples an' th' polis." A disbeliever himself, he says the one who believes should act according to his belief: "Now, I don't believe th' Lord iver commanded even a Mormon f'r to do annything so foolish [as to marry as many women as he wants], an' if he did he wudden't lave th' command written on a pie-plate an' burrid out there at Nauvoo, in Hancock country, Illinye." But Dooley draws an analogy with his friend Hadji Mohammed, whose many wives are accepted and thus points out the inconsistency of western morality (*Philosophy*, 109-14).

"Marriage and Politics" offers comment on another kind of prejudice, that the big jobs are held by married men and the clerkships by bachelors. Dooley says that a politician always marries above his station, but his wife stays where she is, having little opportunity for being educated after she begins rearing a family; and the husband "goes by like a fast thrain by a whistlin' station." Politics is the poor man's college, says Mr. Dooley, and he tells the story of his friend O'Leary whose wife helped him become alderman but, with his advancement, found herself beyond her social capacity when they moved to the boulevard. The husband, too, realized her limitations when he refused a nomination to Congress (*Philosophy*, 141-47).

Incompatibility in marriage becomes the topic of "Home Life of Geniuses," in which Dooley observes that many a man has as his first bride the Day's Work, which has "broke up more happy homes thin comic opry." It becomes a bigger problem for a woman married to a genius, and especially a member of the Parnassian school of French poets. Dooley has been reading the memoirs of one of these, whose devotion to his objective poetry caused him to break a soup plate over the head of his wife while she was unobjectively rocking the baby (*Observations*, 157-63). In "Money and Matrimony," Dooley takes up the argument of a federal judge who said that a man could marry on twenty-five dollars. Dooley recalls the old days when "we looked on mathrimony as a dhraft on posterity, as Mark Hanna wud say, an' not as an invistmint," but he recognizes that wealthy people, in a position to consider the advantages of further alliance with wealth, have different standards (*Observations*, 65–69).

Under the heading of "Rights and Privileges of Women," Dunne phrased as his leading question the definition of "woman's rights": "What does a woman want iv rights whin she has priv'leges?" Explaining the distinction, he says that the pope, emperors, kings, and women have privileges. But for himself, rights are often wrongs turned inside out: "We have th' right to be sued f'r debt instead iv lettin' th' bill run, which is a priv'lege. We have th' right to thrile be a jury iv our peers, a right to pay taxes an' a right to wurruk. . . . Th' constichooshion guarantees me th' right to life, but I die; to liberty, but if I thry bein' too free I'm locked up; an' to th' pursoot iv happiness, but happiness has th' right to run whin pursood, an' I've niver been able to three her yet." With the way women are relieved of responsibilities such as making laws, he concludes, "If I cud fly d'ye think I'd want to walk?" (*Observations*, 253–54).

Dunne took the opportunity of discussing George Meredith's ideas on short marriage contracts to recount the history of a married man, who begins humbly to win the girl of his dreams, then after matrimony slides into content with himself and his bad habits, only to wake up on his wife's reminder after five years that the contract is up; he then decides to mend his ways in order to keep his wife. But Mr. Dooley, while promoting the advantages of this check on one-sided contentment, says, "In me heart I think if people marry it ought to be f'r life" (*Dissertations*, 43–48). In "The American Family," Dunne reflected on the fear expressed by President Eliot of Harvard that the American college population does not reproduce, and likened Harvard graduates to jackasses, which are also dying out (*Dissertations*, 137–41).

"Corporal Punishment" becomes more complicated as an issue than does "Short Marriage Contracts," because Mr. Dooley recognizes that there are many kinds of violence. At the same time, he does not fear the existence of very much wife-beating in this country: "An American lady is not th' person that anny man but a thrained athlete wud care to raise his hand again' save be way iv smoothin' her hair." Among those women who do accept violence, however, he finds that few ever complain, and that divorces do not proceed from that issue. Of the other types of coercion, many go unrecognized as such: a man "may not beat her with a table-leg, but he coerces her with his mind. He can put a savage remark to th' pint iv th' jaw with more lastin' effect thin a right hook. He may not dhrag her around be th' hair iv her head, but he dhrags her be her sympathies, her fears, an' her anxieties. As a last raycoorse he beats her be doin' things that make her pity him." Extending the question of violence to governments, he says, "Th' fav'rite pastime iv civilized man is croolty to other civilized man," such as the Southerner who lynches black men. The only habit, Dooley contends, that a man or a government ought to pray against acquiring is cruelty. Nor does it work. He recalls having been beaten by a sadistic schoolmaster during his days attending an Irish hedgeschool, and found that the beating accomplished nothing but a resentment of the master, a resentment he harbors to this day. The problem does not belong only to the past, however: "Whiniver I hear iv a big six-fut school-teacher demandin' that he be allowed to whale a thirty-two-inch child I feel like askin' him up here to put on th' gloves with Jeffreys. Whin a govermint or a man raysorts to blows it shows they're ayether afraid or have lost their timpers." When Hennessy repeats the old maxim about sparing the rod and spoiling the child, Dooley sees that use of the rod spoils the entirety of civilization, for the attitudes and the damage affect many: "don't spare th' rod an' ye spile th' rod, th' child, an' th' child's father" (*Dissertations*, 221–25).

In "Divorce," the first piece in *Mr. Dooley Says,* Dooley continues the discussion of "Marriage and Politics" about the successful man who bypasses his wife, except this time the analogy is drawn with a businessman. At the conclusion of the story Dooley cites the objections of Father Kelly, who knows that there are no others than ill-mated couples, just as friendship is a kind of suspension bridge between quarrels: "Th' soft answer don't always turn away wrath. Sometimes it makes it worse." Between opposing viewpoints, Dooley can be sure of one thing: the parents divorcing should be given into the custody of the children because "they'd larn thim to behave" (*Says,* 1–13).

In "Woman Suffrage" Dunne returns to the problem of rights of women. At first he agrees with Hennessy that women should stay at home tending the babies, but then he adds, "A baby is a good substichoot f'r a ballot, an' th' hand that rocks th' cradle sildom has time f'r anny other luxuries." He contends that if women would organize a hundred thousand strong, politicians would seek their vote; but they cannot achieve suffrage until they use force, marching in Washington and fighting for it. A person must not ask for rights because "A right that is handed to ye f'r nawthin' has somethin' th' matther with it" (*Says*, 25–39). Dunne thus looked ahead to the Nineteenth Amendment, which was ratified in 1920.

On a proposed bachelor tax, which Dunne compared with a dog license, he expanded on the rights and privileges of bachelors. "Th' marrid men start all th' wars with loose talk when they're on a spree. But whin war is declared they begin to think what a tur-rble thing," Mr. Dooley says. As for the sentiment of women, he adds, " 'Tis a fine idee iv th' ladies that men are onhappy because they have no wan to darn their socks an' put buttons on their shirts. Th' truth is that a man is not onhappy because his socks ar-re not darned but because they ar-re. An' as f'r buttons on his shirt, whin th' buttons comes off a bachelor's shirt he fires it out iv th' window. His rule abut clothes is thurly scientific. Th' survival iv th' fit, d'ye mind. Th' others to th' discard." Women would be shocked at the condition of his room, with nothing but oilcloth and his clothes on the floor, and because " 'tis so long since me bed was made up that it's now a life-size plaster cast iv me." But, he declares, bachelors are bachelors because they cannot make a choice among all the lovely women: "we hate to bring th' tears into th' eyes iv others iv ye be marryin' some iv ye" (*Says*, 40–49).

Mr. Dooley's last word on the women's vote appeared in *Liberty* magazine, after he and Hennessy observed a parade of women, marching in the rain to the polls and looking fetching to the eye of any man. Dooley says, "By dad, I wudden't walk a block in a storm like this to sell me vote, lave alone get it." With all their lovely efforts he finds no change in voting patterns, because the women tended to vote the same way the men did; nor has there been any kind of political house cleaning. Hennessy, however, makes the occasion a family reunion and earns more respect from O'Brien because he now has fifteen family votes to deliver, rather than the earlier three or four. Still,

Mr. Dooley respects the power which women have always had without knowing it (*Liberty,* May 22, 1926).

Dunne turned his attention, also, to the problems of maintaining personal health. "The Grip" tells how to keep cheerful while battling the flu (*Hearts,* 30-34), and in "One Advantage of Poverty" he observes that the poor man has the privilege of being sick in private. A case diagnosed as "peritclipalitickipan-tilitisitis" means chicken bone in the throat (*Observations,* 141-46). Between Christian Scientists and Dock Cassidy, Dooley says, there is the question "whether ye want to be threated like a loonytic or like a can iv presarved vigitables" (*Opinions,* 3-9). Under the heading "Banting," Dooley resists losing weight, but the title officially honors Sir Frederick Grant Banting (1891-1941), co-discoverer of insulin, who later (1923) won a Nobel prize in medicine (*Dissertations,* 27-32). In "Drugs" Dooley tells about the leisureliness of the doctor's visit, his discussion of everything except the illness, and his wondering why "ye can always read a doctor's bill an' ye niver can read his purscription" (*Says,* 89-99). Dooley gives a sample of such a prescription in "Going to See the Doctor," and imagines having the prescription filled at the bank. Dock O'Leary made a mistake with Grogan, having given the chloroform too early; Dooley says, "He shud've give it to him with th' bill" (*Will,* 114-30).

Hennessy's inquiry, "What's a breakfast food?" prompts Dooley to note the impact of oats in advertisement, poetry, and art. His friend explains dry cereal as "a kind iv scientific oatmeal," but Dooley protests that science has extracted the meal. He asks to be passed the ink because "Who iver heerd iv atin' blottin' pa-aper without ink?" (*Dissertations,* 169-73).

Occasionally Dunne wrote on human characteristics under topical headings: "On Pride" (*Liberty,* April 3, 1926); "On Charity" (*Peace,* 187-91); and "Avarice and Generosity" (*Observations,* 255-60). The essays on the problems of aging reveal some surprises, for his essay on "Youth," though it confronts the impact of short skirts and women's legs, concentrates instead on the sprightliness of grandparents of his own generation (*Liberty,* February 20, 1926). The early essay entitled "Old Age" actually deals with the sport of ice skating (*Hearts,* 149-53). On the topic of old age itself, however, Dunne demonstrates his superb wit in an essay surveying the comparative decades of life and speaking of some of his present consolations, such as having "th' full value iv me nickel out iv th' heartless monopuly be holdin' th' car while I get down wan leg at a time." But he likes best to give advice and watch people get into trouble when they follow it: "Manny a man that cudden't direct ye to the dhrug store on th' corner whin he was thirty will get a respictful hearin' whin age has further impaired his mind" (*Will*, 61-70).

Often Dunne's topical essays are of lasting value. For example, "The Union of Two Great Fortunes" (*Hearts*, 234-39), a humorous view of a society wedding, no doubt loses some of its impact when the distinct personalities involved can no longer be recognized except by historians; an incident, rather than a topic, proves less enduring as more incidents accumulate in human history. A union to improve the race, however, has lasting merit; and Dooley begins his discussion of eugenics with saying "manny topicks ar-re now discussed at th' fam'ly fireside that a stevedore wud be thrun out iv a barroom f'r talkin' about in th' reign of Queen Victorya an' Grover Cleveland." Controlled breeding strikes Hogan as bad taste, and he varies Longfellow's "Psalm of Life" to say that "th' lives iv gr-reat men all remind us iv a list iv th' maladies iv th' outpatients at a madhouse," especially when treated by historians who would rather discuss Lincoln's grandmother than the Gettysburg Address (*Liberty*, June 26, 1926). Clearly, history proves either that the great are those who rise above their origins, or that they were never great.

Desire and the point of view may be said to accomplish great things, a fact Dooley observed early in "The Optimist," concerning a person who survives Chicago's hot weather in fine spirits because he reminds himself it is good for the crops (*Hearts*, 170-74). Though he was not a farmer, Dunne dealt with the problems of farmers in the very last essay he wrote (*Liberty*, July 3, 1926).

What came from professional educators often startled Mr. Dooley with its remoteness from common sense. One instance was the pronouncement by a Chicago university professor that many kinds of lies can be explained psychologically and are not really lies. Dooley and Hennessy agree that they know when they are lying, not that a lie comes from something in the subconscious (*Opinions*, 87-90). The education of the young evokes from Mr. Dooley a tale of his having visited a progressive kindergarten, where the children learn in school what they are licked for learning in the back yard. The teacher explains, "We don't believe in corporeal punishment. School shud be made pleasant f'r th' childher. Th' child who's hair is bein' pulled is larnin' patience, an' th' child that's pullin' th' hair is discovrin' th' footility iv human endeavor." Dooley sees these faults carried all the way up to the College of Speechless Thought, where the professor says that "if th' dates iv human knowledge must be rejicted as subjictive, how much more must they be subjicted as rejictive if, as I think, we keep our thoughts fixed upon th' inanity iv th' finite in comparison with th' onthinkable truth with th' ondivided an' onimaginable reality." Dooley recognizes also its opposite, "the College iv Thoughtless Speech," but he loses his argument when he cites himself as an example of the virtues of the old system. Hennessy says that's what worries him (*Philosophy,* 243–49).

The essay "Colleges and Degrees" had its origins not among educators but in an address by Associate Justice Brewer at the Yale Bicentennial in 1901; as Edward Bander writes, Dunne parodied the address.[6] After the address, Dooley says that a doctorate entitles a person "to wear a mother Hubbard in spite iv th' polis," and that American literature does not need a doctor so much as it needs a coroner (*Opinions,* 199–204). Some of Dunne's finest comments on academia, however, can be found in his essay on football for *Liberty* magazine (February 13, 1926).

Perhaps the reason Dooley survives was best expressed by Paul Sayre: "Hatred of hyprocrisy in every form is perhaps the vital force in all of Mr. Dooley's criticisms of men and matters. It is the moral equilibrium that enables Dooley to deal with varied subjects fairly, with complete dignity from his point of view, and with the cheerful freshness of all his thoughts."[7]

CHAPTER 6

Mr. Dooley Endures

THE thirty-odd years which span the Dooley essays brought into existence exciting developments for the future: in 1893 Karl Friedrich Benz and Henry Ford built motor cars; in 1895 Wilhelm Röntgen discovered X-rays, Marconi invented the radiotelegraph, Auguste and Louis Lumière invented the movie camera, H. G. Wells wrote *The Time Machine*, and Sigmund Freud and Josef Breuer wrote *Studies in Hysteria*; in 1896 Antoine Henri Becquerel discovered radioactivity in uranium; and in 1897 Joseph John Thomson discovered the electron; in 1898 Wells wrote *War of the Worlds*; in 1903 the Wright brothers made the first powered flight; in 1905 Albert Einstein published the "Special Theory of Relativity"; in 1907 Henri Bergson published his *Creative Evolution*, and Ivan Pavlov made his famous studies in conditioned reflex; in 1912 Victor Franz discovered cosmic rays; among 1913's several scientific developments, Niels Henrik Bohr presented his theory of atomic structure, and Hans Geiger developed his radium counter; in 1914 Robert Hutchins Goddard began his rocket experiments, and the first open-heart surgery on a dog was performed by Alexis Carrel; in 1917 Carl Jung published his *Psychology of the Unconscious*.

During this period also occurred the sinking of the *Titanic* (1912), the discovery of the Piltdown man (also 1912 but not proved a hoax until 1953), and the opening of the Panama Canal in 1914, the same year as the beginning of World War I. The Constitution was amended radically four times, with Articles 16 through 19 establishing the income tax, prohibition, and women's suffrage. In the decade of the twenties, the first commercial radio station was opened, simultaneously with the invention of television (1920), Tutankhamen's tomb was discovered (1922), Joseph Stalin rose to power (1924), the Scopes Trial on evolution began in Tennessee (1925), and Robert Goddard flew the first liquid-fuel rocket (1926). Dunne stopped writing just before Charles Lindbergh flew across the Atlantic Ocean (1927).

I   *Essays of Lasting Importance*

Into this kind of perspective must be placed Dunne's "Mr. Dooley" essays, especially as they recorded the social—even more so than the scientific—impact of these developments. The era of rapid change was inaugurated with the Chicago Fair, or the World Columbian Exhibition, as it was formally known (1893); Dunne wrote "On the Midway" to express for many the opportunities presented by this and succeeding spectacles of similar nature. The people react, predictably, with as much skepticism, indifference, and boredom as awe. Dooley says, for example, "Th' printin'-press isn't wondherful. What's wondherful is that annybody shud want it to go on doin' what it does" (*Opinions*, 133–41). Sturdy qualities of independence, ego, and self-preservation act as strong bumpers against "future shock."

On the subject of progress in general Dunne wrote "Machinery," but the saving grace of this and other essays—once more—is that Mr. Dooley maintains his usual reductionism and skepticism; for the saving of mankind will be in its refusal to be overwhelmed. Moreover, Dunne could recognize how quickly the opening statement, "Niver befure in th' histhry iv th' wurruld has such pro-gress been made," can become exceedingly trite. At the ordinary human level, Mr. Dooley finds "a taste iv solder in th' peaches," though they were scientifically improved; and he knows that science has done little to improve him: "amidst all these granjoors here am I th' same ol' antiquated combination iv bellows an' pump I always was. Not so good. Time has worn me out. Th' years like little boys with jackknives has carved their names in me top. Ivry day I have to write off something f'r deprecyation." To sum it up, he says, "Mechanical science has done ivrything f'r me but help me." He lists several remarkable developments and the fate of the developers which their ingenuity did not forestall. Extending the discoveries to union with matters of the cosmos, Mr. Hennessy wants to know what Dooley thinks of the man who has announced himself and the Lord as partners in a coal mine. Dooley asks, "Has he divided th' profits?" (*Observations*, 213–19).

On the other hand, social progress seemed always to continue its rearward trek, and many magazines and newspapers made their livings by intentionally alarming the public. The title of Dunne's essay, "National Housecleaning" parodies *Good House-keeping* magazine, and the essay accents our puritanic instincts to root out faults. By contrast, Dooley says, "A Frinchman or an Englishman cleans house be sprinklin' th' walls with cologne; we chop a hole in th' flure an' pour in a kag iv chloride iv lime" (*Dissertations*, 257-62).

As for theories of the construction of the universe, Mr. Dooley in "The Intellectual Life" rendered his verdict: "I dismiss with a loud laugh th' theory that [the world] was created in six days. I cud make such a poor wurruld as this in two days with a scroll saw. Akelly preposterous is th' idee that it wasn't made at all, but grew up out iv nawthin'. Me idee is that th' wurruld is a chunk iv th' sun that was chipped off be a collisyon with th' moon, cooled down, an' advertised f'r roomers. As to its age, I differ with th' Bible. Me own opinyon iv th' age iv th' arth is that it is about twenty-eight years old. That is as far as I go back" (*Disserations*, 107-12). The same topic could appear in an unexpected place. Writing on the American stage, Dunne listed several possibilities of works for adaptations to drama. All are extremely entertaining Dooley witticisms, among which he expects soon the bible "undher th' direction iv Einstein an' Opperman" (*Philosophy*, 223-28).

With allusion to George Ade, Mr. Dooley calls a newspaper article "On the Descent of Man" a "fable in slang," his term for scientific language. Dooley says he always knew that man is better than the other animals because of what is in his head. Darwin came along and "made a monkey iv man," showing that we have lost our tails in the bamboo trees "where our fam'ly had spint so many happy millyons iv years," from which we came down to earth to be men. Having lost his tail, our ancestor lost at once "his manes iv rapid thransit an' his aisy chair," and the "old gintleman" had to go to work. Monkeys have been laughing at people ever since. But Dooley sees the descent theory as an improvement over the earlier idea that man is "a fallin' off fr'm th' angels." Another theory that man has descended from the jumping shrew he finds insulting to the earlier ancestors, such as the lobster, the oyster, the jelly fish, all the way back to the microbe, "an' befure that th' viggytables, an' befure thim th' mud at th' bottom iv th' sea" (*Will*, 81–91).

Dunne continued this topic in 1926, when Mr. Dooley announced that the Scopes trial had "found Darwin guilty, an' voted to hang him th' nex' time he set foot in Chattanooga." He recognizes in Darwin a superiority over contemporary scientists, for Darwin at least wrote " 'mebbe' or 'p'raps' afther ivry line." Of the transfers among species, he explains, "Life was more promiscus in thim days thin it is now, an' it was a wise boa consthrictor that knew its own father." He learns now that the body is mostly water and that "Hootch an' hormones makes life what it is." The descent from the Cro-Magnon man means a terrible drop "to to' lower ordher iv mammals an' invertebrates that infest th' Capitol at Wash'nton at prisint" (*Liberty*, May 1, 1926).

Spiritism as a science, as distinguished from spiritualism as a religion, began with the rappings of the Fox sisters in Hydesville, New York, in 1848. It spread to England, where, in 1882, the Society for Psychical Research was founded with a similar society founded in 1885 in the United States. The society in Europe enrolled many members famous in literature and science, including William James, Henri Bergson, Gilbert Murray, and Camille Flammarion. The American society's motto was Gladstone's statement: "Psychical research is the most important work which is being done in the world—by far the most important." These developments, too, Dunne took into account in "Things Spiritual," which evidences a great deal of knowledge. He begins with the discovery of the weight of the human soul and uses it as his theme, knowing that people would fear for their own esteem to have their souls weighed. Without naming Bergsonian time, he comments on it, saying that "Scales an' clocks ar-re not to be thrusted to decide annything that's worth deciding." He discusses himself in terms of multiple identities, saying "to me I'm a millyon Dooleys an' all iv thim sthrangers to ME," and in this refers to ideas publicly prominent from such works as Madame H. P. Blavatsky's *Secret Doctrine* (1888), in explanation of the Linga-Sharîri of Hindu philosophy, and in P. D. Ouspensky's *Tertium Organum* (1912). The astronomer Percival Lowell had published *Mars and Its Canals* (1906), and Dooley explains faith by citing the discoveries of

Columbus and Lowell. He ends the discussion by recognizing the psychic phenomena of ghosts and of telepathy, with the latter known to him through a Spiritualist friend (*Says*, 123–33).

II   *The Structure of the Essays*

Anything threatening in the environment Dooley could reduce to terms by which people could handle it; anything remote he brought near, making the affairs of the world the affairs of Archey Road. His topics ranged from the far past in such Greek heroes as Miltiades, into the nineteenth century in his Irish origins, and into the immediate past in essays such as "Times Past" and "A Winter's Night," both of which can be read for sheer nostalgia. The latter begins like a novel set in the 1890s: "Any of the Archey Road cars that got out of the barns at all were pulled by teams of four horses, and the snow hung over the shoulders of the drivers' big bearskin coats like the eaves of an old-fashioned house on the blizzard night" (*Hearts*, 72–75). "Times Past" recalls now-outlawed election tactics—the use of force, the stuffed ballot box, the withholding of votes for the opposition (in this case the feeding of Schwartzmeister's ballots to Dorsey's goat), and the rise and fall in local politics of one friend who quickly becomes a former friend (*Hearts*, 50–55).

The structure of the essays reveals why Dunne never succeeded in a sometimes-tendered ambition to write a novel or a play; for the qualities of both those art forms, and to a certain extent, their techniques, appear in random selections. One other type of art Dunne essayed, for which he seems to have been given no recognition by critics, is the tall story. "The Great Hot Spell" (*Hearts*, 180–84), in great purity of form, is a tall story. Throughout the essays, the use of dialect varies, its inconsistency perhaps reflecting typesetters' difficulties as much as Dunne's lack of commitment to it. *Haut finance*, for example, appears as "hawt finance" in one essay and as "ho finance" in another. Dunne's careful use of the subjunctive in the midst of dialect— not the impossibility of Dooley's knowing about a particular person or topic—betrays Dooley's origins in the mind of a master of language.

The structure of the essays can be seen, generally, to move through several distinct stages: (1) a "generating circumstance," in which an item in the newspaper or a comment by Hennessy begins the discussion; (2) Dooley's monologue, beginning with opposing views of a given issue presented with heavy irony so that blind prejudices are exposed as ignorant while sounding intelligent or at least popular; (3) a "reversal," in which Dooley continues the monologue but his own moderate view emerges; (4) a conclusion in which Mr. Hennessy confirms, rejects, or moderates as necessary. Often, especially in the example of a national or international issue, the "reversal" turns the discussion to a personal example in Dooley's memory and/or on Archey Road. In the conclusion, Hennessy offers a comment in the form of a brief penultimate paragraph, usually composed of a single sentence. Dooley then makes the last comment in the last paragraph, also extremely brief; and this last comment acts as a "punch line." The epigrammatic nature of the conclusion has rendered many of these popular for quotation, but the epigrams may actually occur in any part of the essay. Throughout the several hundred essays, Dooley specializes in imaginative flights with lists of exaggerated examples of human fallacies.

III   *Mr. Dooley and the Other Arts*

Besides the eight volumes which Dunne prepared of the Dooley essays, Elmer Ellis's *Mr. Dooley at His Best* (1938), and Edward Bander's *Mr. Dooley on the Choice of Law* (1963), already mentioned—two other outstanding collections have been edited by Louis Filler: *Mr. Dooley: Now and Forever* (1954) and the *World of Mr. Dooley* (1962). The former contains two essays, "Education" and "The Monroe Doctrine," which Dunne did not anthologize and which appeared in the pirated edition *What Dooley Says* (1899). The latter contains six standard-English essays which Dunne wrote for *American* magazine. Both volumes offer excellent introductory essays by Filler, and these stand as possibly the best available among short surveys of the life and work of Finley Peter Dunne. In addition, Robert Hutchinson has brought out *Mr. Dooley on Ivrything and Ivrybody* (1963), reprinting a hundred or so essays.

Many volumes on humor contain some selections of Dunne's work. Arthur P. Dudden edited *The Assault of Laughter: A Treasury of American Political Humor* (1962), reprinting twenty-one of the Dooley essays along with excerpts from the work of several other writers, such as David Ross Locke, Mark

Twain, Ambrose Bierce, and H. L. Mencken. Later, writing
Pardon Us, Mr. President (1976), the same author included a
"Mr. Dooley" section. In general the anthologies on humor which
contain sections devoted to Dunne testify to the continuing
popularity of the Dooley pieces. But Mr. Dooley also appears in
unexpected places, such as the collection *Give Me Yesterday*
(1975) by Lester S. Levy, in which Levy reprints with music the
popular "Mr. Dooley" song.

Readers of James Joyce (1882–1941) will recognize in Dunne's
work several constructions which have become better known as
Joycean. In Joyce's *Ulysses* (1922), for example, Leopold Bloom
puns on "poached eggs on toast" when he remarks of Howard
Parnell, "Poached eyes on ghost" (*U*, 165); but Dooley said it
first, when Dunne was writing about microbes "with eyes like
pooched eggs" (*Opinions,* 5). Joyce had his Stephen Dedalus
look at the mystic poet A. E. (George Russell), remember that he
owed A. E. some money, and think "A.E.I.O.U."; but Dooley had
earlier described an aged millionaire approaching Newport in his
yacht, inquiring, "An' is that where Mr. A.E.I.O.U. an' sometimes
W. an' Y. Belcoort lives an' has his bein'?" (*Opinions,* 14–15).
Dunne and Joyce draw upon a background in Irish folklore which
makes several details the property of the people, and not any
writer exclusively, for example, turning a picture to the wall or
using a potato cure against rheumatism (which Joyce used in
place of the magical herb "moly" in *Ulysses*). Dunne was fond of
turning king's titles into Dooley's dialect, so that he spoke of
Cousin George as "Dooley the Wanst"; and on his return from
Ireland Dunne wrote "Americans Abroad," saying that William
Waldorf Astor, in his applying for British citizenship, had
"renounced fealty to all foreign sovereigns, princes an' poten-
tates an' especially Mack th' Wanst, or Twict [should McKinley
be elected to a second term as president], iv th' United States an'
Sulu an' all his wur-ruks" (*Philosophy,* 22). Joyce adapted Mack
the Wanst to his Mark, referring to him, for example, as "Moke
the Wanst" (*FW* 372.04).[1]

The most striking comparison between Dunne and Joyce,
however, concerns the use of language, for Dunne's bilingual
puns provide excellent background for Joyce's multilingual puns;
what Walter Blair called "Dooleymorphisms" occasionally call to
mind Joyce's verbal polymorphisms and portmanteau words.

Perhaps the best of these occurs in "Insanity as a Defense." Here the doctor testifies, "He suffered fr'm warts whin a boy, which sometimes leads to bozimbral hoptocoliographophilloplutomania or what th' Germans call tantrums."[2]

Joyce was interested in pairs of opposites, of which Dooley and Hennessy provide an excellent example; and he introduced the two of them into *Finnegans Wake* in the Wellington episode in which he refers, as did Mr. Dooley, to the reputed saying of the Duke of Wellington about the playing fields of Eton. In this scene, the old woman Kate as janitrix and guide conducts visitors through a museum and points out pictures of the Battle of Waterloo and other Wellington memorabilia hung on the walls: She says, "This is hiena hinnessy laughing alout at the Willingdone. This is lipsyg dooley krieging the funk from the hinnessy. This is the hinndoo Shimar Shin between the dooley boy and the hinnessy" (*FW* 10.4-7).

Joyce was still in Dublin when Dunne visited there in 1899 and must have read reports of Dunne's visit, of which Elmer Ellis writes, "His reputation had preceded him there, and at his hotel in Dublin reporters called to see Mr. Dooley. To one who asked how Mr. Dooley liked Ireland, Dunne replied: 'You may say Mr. Dooley felt at home when he arrived in Dublin for the first time since he left Chicago.' "[3]

There is evidence that Joyce continued to read Dunne's work. The war in Europe put Joyce on the defensive for his pacificism and he left Austrian Trieste in 1915 to go to neutral Switzerland; he wrote his irritation with the war into a poem called "Dooleysprudence," a parody of the "Mr. Dooley Song," in which he declared his opposition. Among several approximations to Dooley's work, Joyce's fifth stanza, for example, begins,

> Who is the man who says he'll go the whole and perfect hog
> Before he pays the income tax or licence for a dog,[4]

and reflects details from Dunne's essay "The Bachelor Tax," which appeared in *Mr. Dooley Says* (1910).

Joyce's attention to Dunne gives Dunne just one more kind of immortality, as evidenced in the next stage of the Dooley-Dooleysprudence history. The two poems were revived on Broadway in 1975 in the award-winning play *Travesties* by Tom

Stoppard, in which Joyce as a character in the play recites twenty-two lines from his poem, introducing it as "my version of Mr. Dooley."[5]

Perhaps the greatest irony touching the lives of Dunne and Joyce involved publishing. To Dunne in 1899 Grant Richards as pirate of *Mr. Dooley in Peace and in War* was nothing more than an unprincipled scoundrel; probably Joyce remained ignorant of this part of Richards' history throughout his negotiations with Richards to publish, beginning in 1904, Joyce's *Chamber Music* poems, next *Dubliners,* and later *A Portrait of the Artist as a Young Man.* Perhaps, also, Dunne had seemed to diminish the importance of his authorship when he withheld his name from the first book, having indicated it only with the signing of his three initials at the close of the "Preface." Fighting bankruptcy and the revolt of his printer, however, Grant Richards did not succeed in publishing for Joyce until 1914, when he brought out *Dubliners.*

In addition to mention in Tom Stoppard's *Travesties,* Mr. Dooley was revived briefly during the Democratic National Convention in 1976 when Ed Asner recited passages from the political essays. Dunne's screenwriting son Philip has, with Martin Blaine, written a drama entitled "Mr. Dooley's America" in which they adapt Finley Peter Dunne's work and use Elmer Ellis's title.

Dooley has always enjoyed popularity with historians. Just as Elmer Ellis found Dunne's essays useful in history classes, so also have others quoted him in their published histories. A flurry of activity among Chicago historians has brought forth three books on Dunne in three years: Charles Fanning's *Mr. Dooley and the Chicago Irish* (1976), Barbara C. Schaaf's *Mr. Dooley's Chicago* (1977), and Charles Fanning's *Finley Peter Dunne and Mr. Dooley* (1978). The first two reprint articles from the Chicago years, many of them here anthologized for the first time, with introductions explaining the backgrounds in Chicago history and other obscure details, such as Irish terms which may elude contemporaries. Fanning's second book is a biographical-historical study which offers excerpts from the Chicago essays and appends a chronology of Dunne's dialect pieces in the *Chicago Evening Post* A fourth book—*Small Town Chicago: The Comic Perspective: George Ade, Finley Peter Dunne, Ring Lardner* (1979)—places Dunne in relationship with two other Chicago humorists. Lest the public return to thinking of Dooley as strictly a Chicagoan and of Dunne as a Chicago humorist, however, comparable work still needs to be done for the years 1900 to 1926. A beginning has been made in William A. Gibson's *Theodore Roosevelt Among the Humorists* (1980) in which the author shows that the critiques of W. D. Howells, Mark Twain, and Finley Peter Dunne provided a needed check on presidential powers and served to protect civil liberties.

The test of all great writing may well be its prophetic qualities, and certainly much of Dunne's work has this quality. Philip Dunne, when collecting his father's memoirs in 1962, asked to be permitted to believe that "if Mr. Dooley had been lurking in ambush, piece loaded and cocked, Mr. Nixon wouldn't have made his 'Checkers' speech at all (*Remembers*, 103-104). Such power, indeed, had the Irish bards who sat next to the king and kept him in check with the threat of their satire. The breakdown of amenities after President Carter's Camp David agreement between the Israelis and the Arabs underscores once more the truth of Dunne's essay on "International Amenities": "Unforchunitly diplomacy on'y goes as far as the dure. It is onable to give protection to th' customer, so whin he laves th' shop th' sthrong arm men iv th' Sinit knocks him down an' takes fr'm him ivrything he got inside an' more too" (*Observations*, 35). Discussing the modern explosive lyddite, Dooley predicted much of what became, in its destruction of defenseless citizens, a reality with the atomic bomb: "I can see in me mind th' day whin explosives'll be so explosive an' guns'll shoot so far that on'y th' folks that stay at home'll be kilt, an' life insurance agents'll be advisin' people to go into th' ar-rmy" (*Philosophy*, 68).

The endurance, as well as the prophetic qualities, of the essays springs from the similarity in human existence throughout the fleeting decades. The problems remain the same; only the customs and manners change—and even those not very much.

Notes and References

Chapter One

1. Elmer Ellis, *Mr. Dooley's America: A Life of Finley Peter Dunne* (New York: Alfred A. Knopf, 1941); cited hereafter as *America.*

2. Throughout the present text, brief parenthetical citations as identified below will indicate the source of the Dunne material being discussed:

Dissertations	*Dissertations by Mr. Dooley* (New York, 1906).
Hearts	*Mr. Dooley in the Hearts of His Countrymen* (Boston, 1899).
Observations	*Observations of Mr. Dooley* (New York, 1902).
Opinions	*Mr. Dooley's Opinions* (New York, 1901).
Peace	*Mr. Dooley in Peace and in War* (Boston, 1898).
Philosophy	*Mr. Dooley's Philosophy* (New York, 1900).
Remembers	*Mr. Dooley Remembers: The Informal Memoirs of Finley Peter Dunne,* ed. Philip Dunne (Boston, 1963).
Says	*Mr. Dooley Says* (New York, 1910).
Will	*Mr. Dooley on Making a Will and Other Necessary Evils* (New York, 1919).

3. Charles F. Fanning, Jr., "Mr. Dooley's Bridgeport Chronicle," *Chicago History* 2:1 (Spring 1972): 47-57.

4. "Mr. Dooley's Troubles," *Chicago History* 5 (1957-60): 104-12.

5. I have not yet found a published copy of the song, the "Mr. Dooley March," or further information on it; however, "Mister Dooley" has been reprinted with music in Lester S. Levy, *Give Me Yesterday: American History in Song, 1890-1920* (Norman: Univ. of Oklahoma Press, 1975), pp. 101-107.

6. Edward J. Bander, ed., *Mr. Dooley on the Choice of Law* (Charlottesville, Va: Michie, 1963), p. 71.

Chapter Two

1. Letter of Philip Dunne to the author, March 12, 1978.

2. See Edward Norman, *A History of Modern Ireland* (London: Allen Lane, The Penguin Press, 1971), p. 14.

3. Georg Mann, "Call for Mr. Dooley," *Eire-Ireland* 9:3 (Autumn 1974): 119-27.

4. See *Mr. Dooley and the Chicago Irish: An Anthology,* ed. Charles Fanning (New York: Arno Press, 1976), pp. 416-20.

5. See Barbara C. Schaaf, *Mr. Dooley's Chicago* (New York: Anchor Press/Doubleday, 1977), pp. 67-70.

6. For a recent, though somewhat exaggerated, view of Irish drinking habits, see Richard Stivers, *A Hair of the Dog: Irish Drinking and American Stereotype* (University Park: Pennsylvania State Univ. Press, 1976).

7. Schaaf, pp. 89-90.

8. Ibid., pp. 79-92.

9. Ibid., pp. 189-92; also Fanning's *Mr. Dooley and the Chicago Irish,* pp. 2-6.

10. Schaaf, pp. 176-221. "Dooley in the Storm" is "The Wanderers" in *Hearts.*

11. Fanning, *Mr. Dooley,* pp. 371-433.

12. William L. Riordon, *Plunkitt of Tammany Hall: A Series of Very Plain Talks on Very Practical Politics,* intro. Arthur Mann. (rpt. New York: E. P. Dutton, 1963).

13. Malcolm Brown, *The Politics of Irish Literature* (Seattle: Univ. of Washington Press, 1972), p. 200.

14. Fanning, *Mr. Dooley,* pp. 409-13; also "On a Plot" (*Peace,* 130-35).

15. Fanning, *Finley Peter Dunne & Mr. Dooley: The Chicago Years* (Lexington: Univ. Press of Kentucky, 1978), pp. 157-62, 213-14.

16. Mann, 125; *Remembers,* p. 33.

17. Lawrence J. McCaffrey, *The Irish Diaspora in America* (Bloomington: Indiana Univ. Press, 1976), p. 84.

18. Fanning, *Finley Peter Dunne,* p. 171.

19. Thomas N. Brown, *Irish-American Nationalism, 1870-1890* (Philadelphia: J. B. Lippincott, 1966), p. 180.

20. Norman, p. 249.

Chapter Three

1. Walter Blair, *Native American Humor* (New York: American Book, 1937; rpt. San Francisco: Chandler, 1960), p. 105.

2. Walter Blair, *Horse Sense in American Humor: From Benjamin Franklin to Ogden Nash* (New York: Russell & Russell, 1942), p. 248. Cited as *Horse Sense.*

3. Interview with Elmer Ellis, November 24, 1978.

4. Norris W. Yates, *The American Humorist: Conscience of the Twentieth Century* (Ames: Iowa State Univ. Press, 1964), p. 62.

5. Bernard Duffey, "Humor, Chicago Style," *The Comic Imagina-*

tion in American Literature, ed. Louis D. Rubin, Jr. (New Brunswick, N.J.: Rutgers Univ. Press, 1973), pp. 207–16.

6. Yates, p. 71.

7. Ibid., pp. 78–79.

8. Franklin P. Adams, "Foreword," *Mr. Dooley at His Best,* ed. Elmer Ellis (New York: Charles Scribner's Sons, 1938), p. xviii; cited hereafter as *At His Best.*

9. Walter Blair and Hamlin Hill, *America's Humor: From Poor Richard to Doonesbury* (New York: Oxford Univ. Press, 1978), p. 385.

10. Finley Peter Dunne, *Mr. Dooley's Philosophy* (New York: Harper, 1906), pp. 27–34, 77–82; cited hereafter as *Philosophy.*

11. Quoted in Elmer Ellis, *Mr. Dooley's America* (New York: Alfred A. Knopf, 1941), p. 109.

12. Kurt M. Stein, "Introduction" by Richard Atwater, *Die Schönste Lengevitch* (New York: Covici, Friede, 1923), pp. 11–13.

13. William L. Riordon, *Plunkitt of Tammany Hall* (New York: E. P. Dutton, 1963). Cited as *Plunkitt.*

14. Stephen Birmingham, *Real Lace: America's Irish Rich* (New York: Harper and Row, 1973), p. 9.

15. Letter, Theodore Roosevelt to Finley Peter Dunne, November 23, 1904. (Theodore Roosevelt Papers, 1878–1919) (Library of Congress).

16. Harry Thurston Peck, *Twenty Years of the Republic, 1885–1905,* pp. 498–502, quoted in John D. Hicks, *The American Nation: A History of the United States from 1865 to the Present* (New York: Houghton Mifflin, 1949), p. 271.

17. Theodore Roosevelt, Letter to Finley Peter Dunne, November 23, 1904. Theodore Roosevelt Papers, 1878–1919 (Library of Congress).

18. Eleanor Randolph, "Mort Sahl Still Kicks Guy on Top," *Chicago Tribune,* rpt. *Des Moines Register,* December 23, 1978, p. 1B.

19. Philip Dunne, letter to the author, March 12, 1978.

20. Homer Croy, *Our Will Rogers* (New York: Duell, Sloan and Pearce, 1953), p. 195.

21. Ibid., pp. 174, 217.

22. Ibid., p. 186.

Chapter Four

1. Ellis, p. 111.

2. See Blair, *Horse Sense in American Humor,* p. 252. Also quoted in Norris W. Yates, *The American Humorist* (Ames: Iowa State Univ. Press, 1964), p. 106.

3. Gerald F. Linderman, *The Mirror of War: American Society and*

the Spanish-American War (Ann Arbor: Univ. of Michigan Press, 1974), p. 12; cited hereafter as *Mirror of War*.

4. Quoted in Marcus M. Wilkerson, *Public Opinion and the Spanish-American War: A Study in War Propaganda* (New York: Russell & Russell, 1932; rpt. 1967), p. 92.

5. Russell A. Alger, *The Spanish-American War* (New York: Harper, 1901), p. 31.

6. Charles H. Brown, *The Correspondents' War: Journalists in the Spanish-American War* (New York: Charles Scribner's Sons, 1967), p. 207; cited hereafter as *Correspondents*.

7. Henry Cabot Lodge, *The War with Spain* (New York: Arno Press and The New York Times, 1970), p. 22.

8. Quoted in John Edward Weems, *The Fate of the Maine* (New York: Henry Holt, 1958), p. 13; cited hereafter as *Fate*.

9. H. Wayne Morgan, *America's Road to Empire: The War with Spain and Overseas Expansion* (New York: John Wiley, 1966), p. 66.

10. Alger, p. 181.

11. In John D. Long, *The New American Navy*, vol. 2 (New York: Outlook, 1903), p. 48; cited hereafter as *Navy*.

12. Johnson Brigham, *Iowa: Its History and Its Foremost Citizens* (Chicago: S. J. Clarke, 1915), p. 649.

13. Louis Filler, ed., *Mr. Dooley: Now and Forever* (Stanford, Calif., Academic Reprints, 1954), p. xiv.

14. Lodge, p. 67.

15. Quoted in John D. Hicks, *The American Nation* (New York: Houghton Mifflin, 1949), p. 331.

16. Elbert Hubbard, *A Message to Garcia and Other Essays* (New York: Thomas Y. Crowell, 1924), p. 7.

17. Lodge, p. 236.

18. James Bryce, "The Historical Causes of the Present War in South Africa," *Briton and Boer: Both Sides of the South African Question* (New York and London: Harper, 1900), pp. 38–44.

Chapter Five

1. Louis L. Snyder, *The Dreyfus Case: A Documentary History* (New Brunswick, N.J.: Rutgers Univ. Press, 1973), p. 74.

2. George E. Mowry, *The Era of Theodore Roosevelt, 1900–1912* (New York: Harper, 1958), p. 70.

3. Edward J. Bander, ed., *Mr. Dooley on the Choice of Law* (Charlottesville, Va.: Michie, 1963), p. 22.

4. Ibid., pp. vii–viii.

5. Louis Filler, ed., *The World of Mr. Dooley* (New York: Collier, 1962), p. 209.

6. Bander, p. viii.

7. Quoted in Bander, p. ix.

Chapter Six

1. I have followed "Joyce industry" custom in citing Joyce sources. Page numbers are given in parentheses for *Ulysses* (New York: Random House, 1961) and page and line numbers for *Finnegans Wake* (New York: Viking, 1939).

2. Bander, p. 25.

3. Ellis, *Mr. Dooley's America*, p. 130.

4. James Joyce, *The Critical Writings*, ed. Ellsworth Mason and Richard Ellmann (New York: Viking, 1959), pp. 246–48.

5. Tom Stoppard, *Travesties* (New York: Grove Press, 1975), p. 49.

Selected Bibliography

PRIMARY SOURCES

1. Books by Finley Peter Dunne

Mr. Dooley in Peace and in War. Boston: Small, Maynard, 1898.
Mr. Dooley in the Hearts of His Countrymen. Boston: Small, Maynard, 1899.
Mr. Dooley's Philosophy. New York: R. H. Russell, 1900.
Mr. Dooley's Opinions. New York: R. H. Russell, 1901.
Observations of Mr. Dooley. New York: R. H. Russell, 1902.

Dissertations by Mr. Dooley. New York: Harper, 1906.
Mr. Dooley Says. New York: Charles Scribner's, 1910.
Mr. Dooley on Making a Will and Other Necessary Evils. New York: Charles Scribner's Sons, 1919.
Mr. Dooley Remembers: The Informal Memoirs of Finley Peter Dunne. Ed. Philip Dunne. Boston: Little, Brown, 1963.

2. Collections of Dunne by Others

Mr. Dooley at His Best. Ed. Elmer Ellis. New York: Charles Scribner's Sons, 1938; rpt. Hamden, Conn.: Archon Books, 1969.
Mr. Dooley and the Chicago Irish: An Anthology. Ed. Charles Fanning. New York: Arno Press, 1976.
Mr. Dooley: Now and Forever. Ed. Louis Filler. Stanford, Calif.: Academic Reprints, 1954.
Mr. Dooley on Ivrything and Ivrybody. Ed. Robert Hutchinson. New York: Dover, 1963.
Mr. Dooley on the Choice of Law. Ed. Edward J. Bander. Charlottesville, Va.: Michie, 1963.
What Dooley Says. Pirated edition. Chicago: Kazmer, 1899.
The World of Mr. Dooley. Ed. Louis Filler. New York: Collier Books, 1962.

SECONDARY SOURCES

1. Books on Finley Peter Dunne

DeMuth, James. *Small Town Chicago: The Comic Perspective: George*

Ade, Finley Peter Dunne, Ring Lardner. Port Washington, N.Y.: Kennikat Press, 1979. Places Dunne in perspective with two other Chicago humorists.

ELLIS, ELMER. *Mr. Dooley's America: A Life of Finley Peter Dunne.* New York: Alfred A. Knopf, 1941; rpt. Hamden, Conn.: Archon Books, 1969. Authoritative critical biography of Finley Peter Dunne.

GIBSON, WILLIAM M. *Theodore Roosevelt Among the Humorists: W. D. Howells, Mark Twain, and Mr. Dooley.* Knoxville: Univ. of Tennessee Press, 1980. Argues that humorous critiques of Roosevelt's presidency provided a needed check on his powers.

FANNING, CHARLES. *Finley Peter Dunne and Mr. Dooley: The Chicago Years.* Lexington: Univ. Press of Kentucky, 1978. Vividly written, with some disregard for accuracy. Chicago backgrounds with excerpts from the essays. Gives the impression that Dunne stopped writing in 1898. Illustrated.

SCHAAF, BARBARA C. *Mr. Dooley's Chicago.* New York: Doubleday, 1977. Reproduces a selection of the Chicago essays with careful introductions.

2. Articles on Finley Peter Dunne

FANNING, CHARLES F. "Mr. Dooley's Bridgeport Chronicle." *Chicago History* 2:1 (1972): 47–57. Some inaccuracies; otherwise a good introduction. Excellent illustrations.

HARRISON, JOHN M. "Finley Peter Dunne and the Progressive Movement." *Journalism Quarterly* 44:3 (1967): 475–81. Good background on Dunne's attitude toward progressivism.

KELLEHER, JOHN V. "Mr. Dooley and the Same Old World." *Atlantic* 177 (June 1946): 119–25. An appreciative study of Dunne's relevance today.

MANN, GEORG "Call for Mr. Dooley." *Eire-Ireland* 9:3 (Autumn 1974): 119–27. Defends the Irishness of Mr. Dooley.

"Mr. Dooley's Troubles." *Chicago History* 5:4 (Summer 1958): 104–12. Recounts Dunne's anxiety about the success of his first books, with letters held by the Chicago Historical Society.

SCHAAF, BARBARA C. "The Man Who Invented Mr. Dooley." *Chicago Magazine* 26 no. 3 (March, 1977), 116–217. Good introductory study of Dunne in Chicago.

SEMONCHE, JOHN E. "The 'American Magazine' of 1906–15: Principle vs. Profit." *Journalism Quarterly* 40:1 (1963): 36–44. Discusses Dunne as one of the founders of *American* magazine.

SILLEN, SAMUEL. "Dooley, Twain, and Imperialism (1898–1903)." *Masses and Mainstream* 1 (December 1948): 6–13. Examines Dunne's and Twaine's opposition to imperialism.

SMITH, JOHN JUSTIN. "Dunne Hit Dimmycrats and Raypublicans." *Chicago Daily News,* July 12, 1976, sec. 2, p. 17.

——. "Misther Dooley Wud Iv Loved the Dimmycrats." *Chicago Daily News,* July 10, 1976, p. 1ff. Dunne's witticisms, especially those applicable to the Democratic convention.

3. Supplementary Sources

ADAMS, FRANKLIN P. "Foreword." *Mr. Dooley at His Best.* Ed. Elmer Ellis. New York: Charles Scribner's Sons, 1938. Excellent explanation of Dunne's rationale for Irish dialect by editor who worked with Dunne.

ALGER, RUSSELL A. *The Spanish-American War.* New York: Harper, 1901. Defensive writing by the Secretary of War.

BIRMINGHAM, STEPHEN. *Real Lace: America's Irish Rich.* New York: Harper and Row, 1973. Not a "scholarly" text, has interesting and informative details about the Irish-born and their descendants.

BLAIR, WALTER, and HILL, HAMLIN. *America's Humor: From Poor Richard to Doonesbury.* New York: Oxford Univ. Press, 1978. History of humor, not much space given to Dunne.

——. *Horse Sense in American Humor: From Benjamin Franklin to Ogden Nash.* New York: Russell & Russell, 1942. Some gross inaccuracies in regard to Dunne's Mr. Dooley.

——. *Native American Humor.* New York: American Book, 1937; rpt. San Francisco: Chandler, 1960. Several references to Dunne, plus two essays, "On the Victorian Era" and "On Books."

BROWN, CHARLES H. *The Correspondents' War: Journalists in the Spanish-American War.* New York: Charles Scribner's Sons, 1967. An excellent and comprehensive treatment of the role of journalism, with excerpts from writing of the time.

BROWN, MALCOLM. *The Politics of Irish Literature.* Seattle: Univ. of Washington Press, 1972. A valuable aid for Dunne's Irish essays.

BROWN, THOMAS N. *Irish-American Nationalism, 1870–1890.* Philadelphia: J. B. Lippincott, 1966. Excellent for background history used in Dunne's Irish essays.

BRYCE, JAMES, et al. *Briton and Boer: Both Sides of the South African Question.* New York and London: Harper, 1900. First essay, "The Historical Causes of the Present War in South Africa," gives much background for the Dooley essays.

CROWE, RICHARD T. "The Legacy of the Canal Irish." *St. Patrick's Day Parade Book.* Chicago: The City of Chicago, 1976. Early Irish history out of which Dunne wrote.

CROY, HOMER. *Our Will Rogers.* Boston: Little, Brown, 1953. A carefully researched biography which had its origins in personal acquaintance with Will Rogers.

DUDDEN, ARTHUR POWER. *The Assault of Laughter: A Treasury of*

Political Humor. New York: A. S. Barnes, 1962. Introduction on Dunne; reproduces twenty-one Dooley essays.

———. *Pardon Us, Mr. President.* New York: A. S. Barnes, 1976. On political humor; contains "Mr. Dooley" section.

HUBBARD, ELBERT. *A Message to Garcia and Other Essays.* New York: Thomas Y. Crowell, 1924. Background information for Dunne's essays. Preface and Apologia explain the history of the "Message."

JOYCE, JAMES. *Ulysses.* New York: Random House, 1961. Shows evidence that Joyce read Dunne.

KRAMER, DALE. *Chicago Renaissance: The Literary Life in the Midwest, 1900–1930.* New York: Appleton-Century, 1966. Mentions Dunne.

LEVY, LESTER S. *Give Me Yesterday: American History in Song, 1890–1920.* Norman: Univ. of Oklahoma Press, 1975. Reprints words and music for the "Mr. Dooley" song.

McCAFFREY, LAWRENCE J. *The Irish Diaspora in America.* Bloomington: Indiana Univ. Press, 1976. Treats Dunne as Chicago Irish.

MOWRY, GEORGE E. *The Era of Theodore Roosevelt, 1900–1912.* New York: Harper, 1958. An authoritative source for Roosevelt and Dunne's treatment of him.

RUBIN, LOUIS D., JR., ed. *The Comic Imagination in American Literature.* New Brunswick, N.J.: Rutgers Univ. Press, 1973. Essay by Bernard Duffy limits Dunne to Chicago.

STOPPARD, TOM. *Travesties.* New York: Grove Press, 1975. Play brings together James Joyce, Lenin, and Tristan Tzara in Zurich. Joyce recites twenty-two lines from his own Mr. Dooley poem.

YATES, NORRIS W. *The American Humorist: Conscience of the Twentieth Century.* Ames: Iowa State Univ. Press, 1964. A comprehensive survey but somewhat inaccurate regarding Dunne; lists as by Dunne two books which were not published.

3. Television Tape

Mr. Dooley and Convention. Washington, D.C.: Democratic National Headquarters, 1976. A tape of approximately twenty minutes, ten of which are on Mr. Dooley, played by Ed Asner.

Index to Essays Cited

This index serves the two purposes of aid in location of Dunne's essays in the collections of his works and in discussions of the essays in this volume. Titles under the "essay source" heading are the abbreviations of his book titles explained in Footnote 2 of Chapter One, page 153, of this volume, except those essays marked *Liberty*, which appeared in *Liberty* magazine, 1926. Parenthetical citations are for Charles Fanning, *Mr. Dooley and the Chicago Irish* (1976); Louis Filler, *Mr. Dooley: Now and Forever* (1954) and *The World of Mr. Dooley* (1962); and Barbara C. Schaaf, *Mr. Dooley's Chicago* (1977).

162

Index